the
VINTAGE TEA PARTY
TREASURY

the VINTAGE TEA PARTY TREASURY
ANGEL ADOREE

ACC ART BOOKS

www.antiquecollectorsclub.com

ISBN: 978 1 85149 799 7

Published in 2015 in North America by ACC Art Books and distributed by
ACC Distribution (6 West 18th Street, Suite 4B, New York, NY10011), a division of
ACC Publishing Group, Sandy Lane, Old Martlesham, Woodbridge, Suffolk, IP12 4SD, UK.

First published in Great Britain in 2015 under the title *Your Vintage Tea Party Journal* (ISBN: 9781784720940)
by Mitchell Beazley, an imprint of Octopus Publishing
Group Limited, Carmelite House, 50 Victoria Embankment, London EC4Y 0DZ
www.octopusbooks.co.uk

This material was previously published in *The Vintage Tea Party Book*,
The Vintage Tea Party Year and *The Vintage Sweets Book*

Copyright © Octopus Publishing Group Limited 2015 | Text copyright © Angel Adoree 2015

A CIP catalogue record for this book is available from the British Library.

Printed and bound in China.

PUBLISHER'S NOTES
The advice in this book is believed to be correct at the time of printing, but the authors and the
publishers accept no liability for actions inspired by this book. This book contains some dishes made with
raw or lightly cooked eggs. It is prudent for more vulnerable people, such as pregnant and nursing mothers,
people with weakened immune systems, the elderly, babies, and young children, to avoid dishes made with
uncooked or lightly cooked eggs. The prep time listed for each recipe represents the amount of time it takes
to complete all stages of the recipe prior to cooking. The total time includes the prep time.

RECIPE CREDIT
The wondrous Caramelized Pomegranate and Carrot Cake on pages 56–57 is reproduced
by permission of Gattina Cheung (http://gattinamia.blogspot.com/)

the VINTAGE TEA PARTY TREASURY

Angel Adoree

ACC ART BOOKS

FOR MY DARLING, DICK

Thank you for giving us our beautiful little girl,
Dorothy Francis Strawbridge. She came into our
lives and blew us away with her soft and
sweet nature. I already know she will melt
our hearts and boss Arthur around!

CONTENTS

Drinks

Craft & Other Essentials

INTRODUCTION

Welcome to *The Vintage Tea Party Treasury*. You are about to embark on a very personal journey capturing all your favourite vintage tea party inspirations. And on your travels you can personalize this book to create an heirloom that I truly hope will be treasured within your family for many a tea party to come!

My Journey

I like old things. Unique one-off items with character and charm. Old-fashioned rituals, manners and ways of life define me. I live and breathe a past time when life was simpler, yet steeped in style and elegance.

I discovered my passion for all things vintage when I was just a few years old. My family is from the East End of London, where I was brought up by ladies whom I considered to be the most beautiful and elegant in all the land! Although their ways were from a now-long-gone era, their mannerisms, customs, styles and values instilled warmth and richness in my life. My open-hearted parents were always throwing soirees when I was younger, and I'm proud to have inherited the hosting gene. We have always worked hard as a family, but we know the importance of family time and this always revolves around food! My early

Above: My dad (centre) playing the Mad Hatter in his school play, 1959.

Top: Me aged 4, 1981.
Bottom: (From left to right) My Mum, Gran and Auntie Pat in a back garden in East London, 1967.

Right: Designer Erdem and the Vintage Patisserie
team at the Cutler and Gross Vintage Store, 2009.

Right: Designer Erdem and the Vintage Patisserie
team at the Cutler and Gross Vintage Store, 2009.

experiences, shared with them around
the dining table, at the kitchen counter
and on many a picnic blanket, are the
source of my passion for entertaining.

During my teens, I started thrifting
at a local car boot sale and became
addicted to hunting down
glamorous old items that, to me,
were valuable remnants of glorious
bygone days. I would buy clothes
that did not fit, tea sets I would not use and
a variety of other items that cluttered up my room and sent
my parents into a spin! In my early twenties, I transformed my addiction
into my first business, called the Angel-A Vintage Experience. I would sell my finds while
spoiling my guests with wonderful food and drink. As I mentioned, hosting is part of my
being and, in 2007, my humble beginnings in vintage hospitality took the natural progression
into a fully-fledged vintage hospitality business. The Vintage Patisserie was born, offering
bespoke vintage parties. I had to pinch myself every day at the fact that I was making people
happy by indulging in my passion!

Below: Launch of The Vintage Tea
Party Year Book, September 2012.

Above: Me at the Galaxy Book Awards, 2011.

In 2010, I was blessed with the opportunity to write *The Vintage Tea Party Book*, in which I could share this passion! The book was very well received and, in 2012, I launched *The Vintage Tea Party Year Book*, which celebrated all the special occasions contained within a single year. Perhaps the baby shower chapter subconsciously had an effect, because in 2013 I had an incredible, life-changing year as I celebrated the birth of my little boy, Arthur Donald Strawbridge. He was the best thing I had ever made and the whole experience made me go rather sentimental! I wanted to write a book that the whole family could enjoy and my nostalgia for old-fashioned sweets led me to write the third beautiful book in the series, *The Vintage Sweets Book*. My partner Dick and I had so much fun working on the book, and the sugar thermometer became very much part of our family!

THE PRESENT

There must have been something in the air while writing the sweetie book as I fell pregnant again! In 2014 Dick and I were blessed with a beautiful daughter, Dorothy Francis Strawbridge. Having two children in two years does keep you on your toes! And, sadly, it did bring the Vintage Patisserie in London to an end. It was the end of an era, one that has supplied me with many treasured memories.

But now a new chapter begins! Dick and I talked long and hard about work–life balance and finally made the decision to buy a little chateau in France to concentrate on vintage weddings, a subject that is very close to both our hearts. We plan to host the first vintage wedding in November 2015. It will be ours!

Left: Family Strawbridge days after the arrival of Dorothy Francis, April 2014.

Below: Chateau de la Motte Husson, my new family home, 2015.

your Journey, your Treasury

This book is designed to help you bring your ideas for vintage-inspired entertaining to fruition. The pages that lie ahead are crammed with my hand-picked all-time favourite recipes and things to make from the Vintage Tea Party series of books, to inspire you and help you refine your party planning, whether you're preparing for an elegant afternoon tea party, a relaxed gathering of your intimates for dinner and dancing the night away, or a chic and showy dinner party. I've included all my very best ideas for entertaining. And I've left oodles of space for you to inscribe your own ideas, inspirations, special family recipes and anything else that tickles your fancy as you develop your unique vision for hosting the perfect vintage tea party. Remember – whatever the size of your party, the occasion, the guest list, the theme or the menu, it is all part of your journey, a precious moment in your life to capture and celebrate to the full. So plan, be prepared, be dressed to kill and enjoy!

'To your perfect tea party. May it bring health, happiness, love and lots of laughter.'

Love Angel ♥

your perfect PARTY vision

MOOD board

ℒℴℭ𝒶𝓉𝒾ℴ𝓃

Whether it's tea for two or two hundred, finding the right location is essential for creating your perfect tea party. As a host and events organizer, I always start by asking myself the following questions:

Who am I hosting? ❧ How many am I hosting? ❧ What first impression am I trying to create? ❧ Do I want to hold the party in a themed building?

Home

Never rule out the most obvious solution. We all know that the most memorable parties are in our friends' homes. This is partly because the host is comfortable and relaxed, which creates that personal magic. There are no worries about closing times or logistics, and it's your home! No other place will emulate that intimacy and openness. If you want the personal touch but have concerns about space, fear not. Think about utilizing outdoor space. Most parties, even tea parties, are not seated. There is a wealth of specialist companies on your doorstep that can help with furniture, marquees, outdoor lighting and heating – most are local businesses with the personal touch and they will work within your budget.

That spare room on top of that great pub that no one knows about

If your home is not the answer, then go exploring. At times like this, I look for a location first: somewhere accessible for everyone is a good starting point. Then, equipped with my favoured lipstick and smile, I go hunting. Bars, restaurants, clubs, pubs, churches, town halls... any venue with character gets a visit. Asking is the key. You'll be surprised at how many places have an upstairs room or a secret back room that is not often used. Try looking around your nearest financial district – areas like these are heaving in the week, but at the weekend are like ghost towns, which is perfect for striking a good deal.

The great outdoors

If the great outdoors is more your cup of tea, then try your local park, the gardens of an exquisite stately home or your local riverside. If you like the idea of hosting a party in the park, there may be some rules and regulations that you will have to follow before you start handing out the cakes, so get in contact with your local authority in advance to ask permission and to see if there are any fees for holding a party there. They may even tell you of some places you don't know about.

On the go

How about having a party on the go? Hire a vintage bus, an old-fashioned double decker, or even a taxi (yes, I have hosted a tea party in a black cab). The only things you'll have to worry about are the food, drink and china, and having a good time. There are many original buses still around that aren't being used. If you're feeling really adventurous, try hosting on a boat or even in an original World War II aircraft. This could be a bit tricky for space, but your party will be talked about for ages!

YOUR LOCATIONS

The first time I bought a tea set, from a local boot fair, I was just 12 years old. I had no use for it, but it was very cheap and rather fabulous. Even at that age I remember thinking 'I can sell it at a later date'. And I did, ten years later! Summer 1990 was the start of my career and I never knew it. 'Thrifting' is still my favourite pastime, so here are a few tips on sourcing the goods to ensure you get the right bits at the right price. Remember: if you like it, get it. You may never come across another one.

Vintage is not a new concept

Throughout the 20th century, many fashion designers took their inspiration from the past. In the 1920s, Jeanne Lanvin created ultra-feminine dresses inspired by the French Second Empire (19th century), which were already then referred to as 'vintage'. In the 1960s and 1970s, Barbara Hulanicki created romantic garments for women, in contrast to the futuristic styles and brightness of the contemporary clothing. Her designs were also described as 'vintage', finding their inspiration in past times.

Be innovative; buy 'against the grain'

If you want to make good investments or find bargains, follow your own creative taste and buy what others don't buy. As long as the quality and decoration are fine, your choice should be quite safe. Even though vintage items are extremely popular at the moment, there are still a great many treasures unfound and untouched. Be adventurous in your choice.

Where to buy

There are plenty of places where you can find vintage items. Antique shops, auction houses (especially generalist uncatalogued sales), car-boot/garage sales, charity shops and internet selling platforms are all good places for buying vintage. The best bargains can be obtained when vintage items are offered outside a 'vintage' context, and thus get a bit lost among other items. Therefore, don't necessarily look for vintage sales, but expand your search and try to spot that special item within a wider remit, as probably no one else will have noticed it.

Condition

Of paramount importance when buying vintage is the condition of the piece. There's no point buying vintage porcelain or glass if you have to spend twice the purchase price to have it restored. Besides, there are very few good restorers and they are often very busy. Watch out for cracks and previous repairs. If you discover the item has been previously damaged, just don't buy it. As vintage items are not that old compared to other antiques, vintage collectors are (more than in any other collecting field) very particular and want the items to be in overall good condition commensurate with their age.

1. A cast-metal, tole and polychrome-painted birdcage, with scroll-turned cresting over a domed body, set with fruiting vine leaves and stylized leaf-trailed borders, 1920s.

2. A black-glazed and parcel-gilt teapot and cover, with a boldly striped globular body and stylized leaf-trailed borders, 1920s.

3. A lustre china teacup and saucer, the trumpet-shaped cup with a broad gilt rim, painted with roses inside, with lobed saucer, 1970s.

4. A small Charlie Chaplin figurine raised on a baluster-turned stem set within a glass-domed cloche, 1930s.

5. Two vintage leather suitcases, inscribed with the owner's initials (V.C.P.), circa 1940s/50s.

6. A black-and-white silk evening dress, with broad-cut decolletage inset with sequins, 1930s.

7. A vintage Union Jack flag, 1940s.

8. A taxidermy owl in a lacquered wood and bevelled glass showcase, circa late 19th/early 20th century.

Furniture

Do you fancy late 1940s American furniture? Do you like 20th-century design, or even pre-war chairs? Designer furniture from the previous century, such as Charles and Ray Eames chairs, have often been 'edited' throughout recent decades. Therefore, where original furniture from the 1930s, 1940s and 1950s might be very expensive to purchase, do consider buying later editions, as these can prove to be far less expensive; when they have acquired a bit of wear and tear, they can have as much impact as the originals.

Vintage clothes

There are many places where you can buy vintage clothes. Bear in mind that an increasing number of auction houses now have a department dedicated to fashion, where you will find not only highly wearable evening dresses, but also a lot of designer clothes at attractive prices. You can mix and match some of these vintage clothes to enhance the stylish effect and create your unique look. If you buy well-known vintage fashion labels, the value should also remain or even go up after a few years, further proving it might be a worthwhile investment.

Porcelain

During the 19th and 20th centuries, porcelain tea services were frequently given to young couples as wedding presents. These were kept at the time in dedicated display cabinets and only used on special occasions. They have therefore survived in huge quantities and are often in very good condition. The market is currently flooded with large sets of tea services dating back to the late 19th and early 20th centuries. Because these porcelain tea services are not very fashionable in the current market, it is definitely the right time to buy and enjoy them.

Silver cutlery

Both solid silver and electroplate cutlery have marks, which can often be misleading. On British electroplated silver, you will find the marks EP, EPNS or EPBM. You can also identify electroplated silver if the base metal is showing through. Electroplated silver is very expensive when bought new, but in a secondary market it can be very good value and is extremely decorative when in good condition. Silver usually bears four or five marks: maker's mark, lion passant, town mark, date letter and, sometimes, a duty mark. Again it is a good time to buy silver – not many young people tend to purchase it, as it can be seen as old-fashioned and needs cleaning.

Tea party checklist

Essentials: Teapots, teacups and saucers, dessert plates, cake plates, cake stands, milk jugs, sugar bowls, glassware and jugs, dessert forks, knives, teaspoons, serving spoons.

Non-essentials: Vintage card games, dominos, draughts (boards and pieces), taxidermy, Union Jack, World War II memorabilia – especially flags, tins, candleholders, gramophones, cameras and anything weird and wonderful that catches your eye!

9 An octagonal lacquered tole box, with ivory ground reserves decorated with Egyptian-inspired scenes and the cover with lotus-blossom motifs, circa 1920–40.

10 A parcel-gilt 'pink' Sadler teapot, with stylized sinuous line motifs on a coral ground, 1970s.

11 A miniature Charlie Chaplin memorabilia doll, featuring Charlie in traditional costume holding an umbrella, 1930s.

12 An Indian metal moulded three-tier travel tazza set, featuring three circular dishes emanating from a hoop, raised on a bell-shaped base, early 20th century.

13 A Victorian electroplate James Deakin egg coddler, of ovoid shape, with chicken cast finial and a triform openwork stand, 1871.

14 A stoneware jelly and potted-meat mould, with a brown-glazed exterior of oval lobed shape raised on a flaring base, 1860s.

Jelly and
Potted
Meat
Mould

CHECKLIST

Happy New Year

COME ONE COME ALL!

You are invited to participate

in our

STREET PARTY

which will be held at:

in honour of:

the party starts at:

don't be late!

WHO'S COMING?

PLANNING PAGES

LET'S GET THE TEA PARTY STARTED!

In my early 20s I bought a ceramic pot with a very pretty pattern on it and used it to serve jam. My grandmother thought this was very odd and explained that my jam pot was actually an egg coddler. I now have a variety of egg coddlers and truly don't know what my life would have been like without them. My favourite is an 1871 James Deakin antique egg coddler that sits proudly in my kitchen, looking after the others.

CODDLED Eggs

PREP
5 minutes
COOKING
5–7 minutes

My favourite fillings:
smoked salmon and chives
baby leaf spinach and truffle oil
pancetta
crumbled feta cheese, a few
capers and a sprig of dill

1 Place the empty coddler(s) in a saucepan and fill the saucepan with cold water until it reaches three-quarters of the way up the side of the coddler(s).

2 Remove the coddler(s) from the saucepan and place the pan of water on the stove over a medium heat. Get your egg(s) ready while waiting for this to reach boiling point.

3 Butter each coddler and season to taste. Add your chosen filling, an egg, a little more butter and then season again. Screw on the lid and transfer the coddler(s) to the saucepan and boil for 5–7 minutes, depending on the size of the egg(s) and how soft you like the yolk.

4 Either eat the egg(s) from their coddlers with a spoon, or remove them carefully and serve them on pretty plates.

'An egg coddler is a porcelain or pottery cup with a lid that is used to prepare a dish called, appropriately enough, coddled eggs. Coddled eggs are very much like poached eggs, except that the egg is cooked inside the coddler. The egg(s) are broken into the buttered coddler, and seasonings are added, if desired. The coddler is then closed with the lid and partially immersed in boiling water for a few minutes. When the eggs are cooked to the desired firmness, the coddler is lifted from the boiling water, the lid removed, and breakfast is served, in a lovely decorated dish.'

*Official quotation from
the egg-coddling community.*

We all know that fruit smoothies are good for us, but if you are not careful they can taste a little too wholesome! Fat-free yogurt and milk reduces the calories and makes the drink a little lighter. To make this drink more substantial and sweet, try adding some banana or honey.

TRIPLe berry SMOOThie

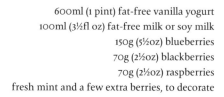

PREP
5 minutes
SERVES
6–8

600ml (1 pint) fat-free vanilla yogurt
100ml (3½fl oz) fat-free milk or soy milk
150g (5½oz) blueberries
70g (2½oz) blackberries
70g (2½oz) raspberries
fresh mint and a few extra berries, to decorate

1 Put the yogurt, milk and berries in a blender and blend on high speed until smooth (about 1 minute).

2 Pour and serve immediately, decorated with extra berries and mint leaves.

The old wives' tale tells us that eating carrots helps your eyesight, but sometimes larger carrots are not so tasty and there are only so many one can eat in a sitting. The apples really lift this drink and the ginger adds a nice little bit of heat. Obviously, such a lovely drink cannot be stirred with anything other than a crisp little baby carrot!

All The better for seeing, you

PREP
5–10 minutes
SERVES 4

10 carrots, roughly chopped
5 apples, cored and roughly chopped
2.5cm (1in) square piece of ginger, peeled
ice cubes
4 baby carrots, to serve

1 Juice the carrots, apples and ginger together and serve in teacups over ice – with a baby carrot to stir, of course.

In my fantasy world, everything would be ruby-coloured. When I make this drink, I taste it first with my eyes. I adore the magnificent deep colour and the earthy taste. Be warned, though: the flavour of the beetroot is so intense that it needs to be tempered with the other fruit and vegetables.

Ruby Deelicious

PREP
5–10 minutes,
plus chilling
SERVES 4

2 cooked beetroots, roughly chopped
2 sticks of celery, trimmed and sliced
6 dessert apples, cored and roughly chopped
5 carrots, roughly chopped
8 radishes, to decorate

1 Juice all the ingredients except the radishes.

2 To make radish roses, cut 4 thin vertical slices around the outside of the radish with a small knife, making sure not to cut all the way through. Repeat this process but each time offset the slice from the previous one, moving closer to the top of the radish. Once this is done, place the radishes in a bowl of iced water and refrigerate for 2–3 hours.

3 Serve the juice in teacups, decorated with a couple of radish roses.

All The Better For Seeing You

Triple Berry smoothie

Ruby Delicious

No afternoon tea is complete without the quintessentially British scone. When served warm with thick clotted cream and luscious strawberry jam, there's nothing quite like it. A fabulous elderly lady once told me that my scones were better than those at the Ritz! They are quick and easy to make, so do give it a go. Here's my basic recipe, but feel free to add other ingredients. Raisins, cinnamon and even chocolate chips would be lovely additions.

CLASSIC SCONE Recipe

PREP
20 minutes
COOKING
16–18 minutes
MAKES 10

70g (2½oz) butter, at room temperature, plus extra for greasing
250g (9oz) plain flour
50g (1¾oz) caster sugar
2 tsp baking powder
¼ tsp salt
125ml (4fl oz) milk
1 large free-range egg, lightly beaten
1 tsp vanilla extract
a little egg and/or milk, for glazing
Strawberry jam and clotted cream, to serve

1 Preheat the oven to 220°C/fan 200°C/gas mark 7. Lightly grease a baking sheet with butter.

2 In a large bowl, mix all the dry ingredients together. Using your fingers, crumble the butter into the mixture until it is evenly distributed, then (still using your hands) gently fold in the milk, egg and vanilla extract. The key is not to mix too much, as mixing will take the air out. Once everything has bound together, separate the mixture into small balls, place these on the prepared baking sheet and glaze with egg, milk or a mixture of both.

3 Bake in the oven for 16–18 minutes, until golden brown. Serve warm with strawberry jam and clotted cream.

A tea loaf is a light, tasty, traditional English cake that has been sweetened with natural fruits, spices and often honey. This is quite a healthy recipe as there is very little fat, and the sweetness comes from the honey and plums (flavours that go beautifully together). It's also easy to make as there is no furious beating – just a few stirs with a wooden spoon and you're done. Serve warm, as it is, or slathered with butter (which then mitigates the healthiness!). I like mine toasted, with a big mug of tea.

PLUM & HONEY Tea bread

PREP
10–15 minutes
COOKING
50–55 minutes
MAKES
a 450g (1lb) loaf

butter, for greasing
200g (7oz) plain flour
1 tsp baking powder
1 tsp bicarbonate of soda
1 tsp ground cinnamon
¼ tsp ground nutmeg
½ tsp salt
175ml (6fl oz) buttermilk or low-fat yogurt
125ml (4fl oz) clear honey
2 tbsp vegetable oil
1 free-range egg, beaten
3 plums, stoned and chopped
60g (2¼oz) walnuts, chopped

1 Preheat the oven to 160°C/fan 140°C/gas mark 3. Grease a 450g (1lb) loaf tin with butter. Sift the flour, baking powder, bicarbonate of soda, spices and salt into a large bowl and mix well.

2 Put the buttermilk or yogurt, honey, oil and egg in a separate bowl and mix until combined. Stir the buttermilk or yogurt mixture into the dry ingredients, then fold in the plums and walnuts.

3 Pour into the prepared loaf tin. The mixture should not fill the tin – leave a gap of about 3cm (1¼in) at the top. Bake for 50–55 minutes or until a wooden pick inserted near the centre comes out clean. Allow to cool a little in the tin and serve while still warm.

Fancy a Morning Tea?

Capture some ideas or your favourite brunch recipes, then look for inspiration to make them look pretty! My top tip: put food in glasses and teacups!

Afternoon tea traditionalists will tell you that cucumber sandwiches are a must on a sandwich platter. Well, to be honest, I find them a tad boring, so I've come up with an Angel Adoree version that is pretty to behold and lovely to eat. You can ring the changes by using a different type of cream cheese and varying the sandwich shape.

CREAM CHEESE & CUCUMBER HEARTS

PREP
10 minutes
MAKES 24

2 small cucumbers
6 slices of soft white bread
15g (½oz) butter, at room temperature
150g (5½oz) cream cheese
salt

1 Top and tail the cucumbers. Using a vegetable peeler, peel 4 strips from the length of each cucumber (one strip on each 'side'). Discard these. Next, peel 12 more strips from the peeled faces of each cucumber (each strip should still have a narrow edge of skin). Cut each strip in half widthways. Set aside.

2 Spread each slice of bread with butter and then with cream cheese, and season with a sprinkling of salt.

3 Lay 4 overlapping strips of cucumber across each slice of bread to cover the cheese. Using a small heart-shaped cutter, cut 4 hearts from each slice of bread. Discard the remains. Serve immediately.

If you are looking for indulgence or just an interesting talking point, the rose petal sandwich could be just the thing. These delicacies may not be everyone's cup of tea, but isn't it good to try something you can't pick up in your local supermarket once in a while? Rose petal sandwiches were popular during the years leading up to World War II. Mine is a slightly more modern take on the classic but, trust me, it's rosy delicious – these sandwiches taste divine, will raise a few eyebrows and look gorgeous, too.

Rose petal sandwiches

PREP
10 minutes,
plus soaking
MAKES 24

60 dried organic rose petals (available on the internet)
few drops of rose essence
25g (1oz) butter, at room temperature
12 slices of soft white bread
6 tsp lavender honey

1 Soak the dried rose petals in a bowl of cold water with the rose essence for 20 minutes (this rehydrates the petals and gives them more flavour), then drain and set aside.

2 Butter the bread, then spread the honey over 6 of the slices.

3 Divide the rose petals between the 6 slices of honeyed bread and top with the remaining bread slices. Cut off the crusts with a serrated bread knife, cut each round diagonally into 4 sandwiches and serve immediately.

HOW TO DRY
EDIBLE FLOWERS

One of my first baking memories is of making rosewater biscuits with my grandmother. I loved the aroma of the rosewater so much that I tried to drink it (I must say, don't try that at home!). My obsession with roses continues now that I'm a grown-up woman, and wherever possible I cook with the pretty little petals, which can be added to salads and cakes, or used as decorations. The bright colours and subtle flavours are marvellous.

If you want to grow edible flowers yourself, be sure never to treat them with pesticides or other chemicals, which are poisonous. Sadly, if you buy flowers from a florist, you should assume that they have been sprayed with these nasties. If you are unable to grow flowers yourself you will, with a little help from the trusty internet, chance upon companies that specialize in dried edible flowers.

Here's a step-by-step guide to drying petals from homegrown flowers.

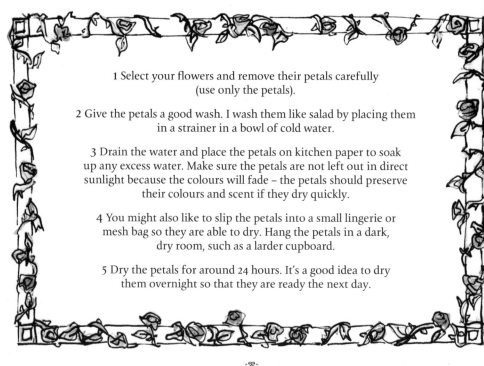

1 Select your flowers and remove their petals carefully
(use only the petals).

2 Give the petals a good wash. I wash them like salad by placing them
in a strainer in a bowl of cold water.

3 Drain the water and place the petals on kitchen paper to soak
up any excess water. Make sure the petals are not left out in direct
sunlight because the colours will fade – the petals should preserve
their colours and scent if they dry quickly.

4 You might also like to slip the petals into a small lingerie or
mesh bag so they are able to dry. Hang the petals in a dark,
dry room, such as a larder cupboard.

5 Dry the petals for around 24 hours. It's a good idea to dry
them overnight so that they are ready the next day.

You can eat the following flowers:

lavender 🌹 carnation 🌹 safflower 🌹 marigold 🌹 cornflower

rose 🌹 mimosa 🌹 violet 🌹 gerbera

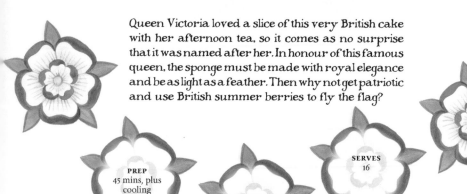

Queen Victoria loved a slice of this very British cake with her afternoon tea, so it comes as no surprise that it was named after her. In honour of this famous queen, the sponge must be made with royal elegance and be as light as a feather. Then why not get patriotic and use British summer berries to fly the flag?

PREP
45 mins, plus cooling

COOKING
15–20 mins

SERVES
16

VICTORIA SPONGE UNION JACK

For the sponge

280g (10oz) unsalted butter, softened

280g (10oz) caster sugar

5 free-range eggs

280g (10oz) self-raising flour

1 tsp vanilla extract

raspberries and blueberries (approx. 400–500g/14–1lb 2oz each), to decorate

For the buttercream

250g (9oz) icing sugar

250g (9oz) unsalted butter, softened

1 tsp vanilla extract

1 Preheat the oven to 180°C/fan 160°C/gas mark 4. Line the base of a 30cm × 46cm (12in × 18in) rectangular baking tray that is about 2.5cm (1in) deep with nonstick baking paper.

2 In a food mixer, cream together the butter and sugar for about 5 minutes until pale and fluffy. With the mixer set on a slow speed, add the eggs one at a time, slipping in a tablespoon of the flour about halfway through to stop the mixture curdling. Sift in the remaining flour and mix until just combined, then stir in the vanilla extract.

3 Tip the cake mixture into the baking tray and spread it evenly with a spoon or spatula. Bake for 15–20 minutes until the top is golden and the sponge is springy to the touch. Leave to cool.

4 Run a knife around the edges of the tin to loosen the sponge, then remove it gently from the tin.

5 To make the buttercream, sift the icing sugar into the cleaned food mixer bowl and mix with the butter for at least 5 minutes. Once it is light and fluffy, mix in the vanilla extract.

6 Spread the buttercream over the cake. You do not want to see any cake, as this will form the base of your flag. Then, using the picture opposite as a guide, decorate the cake with the berries to form a Union Jack.

I often use the internet as a source of recipe ideas and food styling, but only once have I found a recipe that is both unique and so unbelievably tasty that I just want to leave it in its original state. This cake is always a big hit at my parties; I love the twist that the heavenly sweet and fragrant pomegranate arils lend to the classic carrot cake.

Caramelized Pomegranate & Carrot Cake

PREP
30 minutes

COOKING
40–45 minutes

MAKES
18cm (7in) square
cake

1 Preheat the oven to 180°C/fan 160°C/gas mark 4 and grease an 18cm (7in) square baking tin with oil.

2 To caramelize the pomegranate seeds, melt the butter in a pan over a low heat and add the fresh ginger and spices. When their aromas have released, stir in the pomegranate seeds and sugar. Add 15ml (½fl oz) water and slowly reduce to a sticky syrup texture, stirring. Set aside.

3 To make the sponge, combine the flour, bicarbonate of soda, baking powder, salt and sugar in a large bowl. In a separate bowl, whisk the oil, eggs and yogurt together, then combine with the flour mixture, carrot and caramelized pomegranate seeds, being careful not to overmix.

4 Pour the batter into the prepared tin and bake for 40–45 minutes, until it turns golden brown. Test with a toothpick – the cake is done when the pick comes out (almost) clean.

5 Serve in triangles decorated with dollops of cream cheese, baby carrots and a sprinkling of cayenne pepper.

For the sponge

125ml (4fl oz) vegetable oil, plus extra for greasing

150g (5½oz) plain flour

½ tsp bicarbonate of soda

¾ tsp baking powder

pinch of salt

225g (8oz) caster sugar

2 large free-range eggs

3 tbsp natural yogurt

350ml (12fl oz) finely shredded (juicy) carrot

For the caramelized pomegranate seeds

1 tbsp butter

1 tsp diced fresh ginger

½ tsp ground cinnamon

seeds of 1 crushed green cardamom pod

115g (4oz) pomegranate seeds (you can buy these ready prepared in the supermarket, or remove the seeds from roughly 3–4 pomegranates)

2 tbsp caster sugar

To decorate

100g (3½oz) cream cheese

6–8 baby carrots

cayenne pepper

Do you remember the part in *Alice in Wonderland* where Alice meets the Queen of Hearts? There is an explosion of dancing cards, just before the sentence of 'Off with her head'. Well, this tart reminds me of that crazy scene. It is perfect for celebrating a special occasion and will make your guests want to dive in. And while it looks highly indulgent, it is actually incredibly refreshing to the palate after lots of rich, savoury food.

QUEEN OF HEARTS TART

PREP
30 minutes,
plus chilling
COOKING
25 minutes
SERVES 12

For the pastry

500g (1lb 2oz) plain flour, plus extra for dusting

100g (3½oz) icing sugar

250g (9oz) butter, chilled and cubed

2 free-range eggs, beaten

splash of milk (optional)

edible gold lustre spray (available online, optional)

For the raspberry jelly

2 leaves of gelatine

500g (1lb 2oz) frozen raspberries

30g (1oz) caster sugar

1 Sift the flour and icing sugar into a bowl. Rub in the butter. When the mixture resembles breadcrumbs, mix in the eggs, adding some milk if the mixture still looks dry. Bring the dough together into a ball with your hands. Wrap it in clingfilm and chill for 30 minutes.

2 Preheat the oven to 170°C/fan 150°C/gas mark 3½. Roll out the dough on a lightly floured surface and use it to line a 23cm (9in) loose-bottomed fluted tart tin. Use pastry cutters to cut out heart and diamond shapes from the remaining pastry to decorate the tart. Put these on a baking sheet. Cover the pastry-lined tart tin with nonstick baking paper and fill it with baking beans. Bake for 15 minutes, then remove the biscuits from the oven and the paper and

beans from the tart case and bake the case for a further 5 minutes. Allow it to cool. Spray the biscuits with gold lustre, if using, once cool.

3 To make the jelly, cover the gelatine with a little cold water and soak it until softened. Put the raspberries, sugar and 1 litre (1¾ pints) water in a saucepan. Heat the mixture gently until the sugar has dissolved, then simmer for a couple of minutes. Push it through a sieve into a clean pan, heat a little, then add the gelatine leaves (squeezing out the excess water) and leave until dissolved. Strain into a jug and leave to cool.

4 Pour the jelly into the pastry case, refrigerate for 3 hours and top with biscuits to serve.

Bittersweet Chocolate
Pear Cake

Orange Eccles Cakes

'When is a cake not a cake? When it's an Eccles cake!' My grandfather loved saying this each time my gran brought out a plate of these delicious homemade goodies when I visited. He was right, too: an Eccles cake is actually a pastry. I have brought my gran's recipe up to date with the addition of some orange rind. A dredging of sugar on these cakes gives a good crunch.

orange eccles cakes

PREP
25 minutes,
plus soaking
COOKING
10 minutes
MAKES 6

115g (4oz) currants
4 tbsp orange liqueur
finely grated rind of 1 orange
175g (6oz) ready-made puff pastry
plain flour, for dusting
25g (1oz) butter
granulated sugar, for sprinkling
1 free-range egg, beaten
candied peel, to decorate

1 Combine the currants, orange liqueur and rind in a bowl, cover and leave for 24 hours, or until the fruit is plump and has absorbed all the liqueur.

2 Preheat the oven to 180°C/fan 160°C/gas mark 4. Using a rolling pin, roll out the puff pastry on a lightly floured surface until it is nice and thin and then cut into 6 rounds the size of a tumbler, about 6cm (2½in) in diameter.

3 Place a scant teaspoonful of marinated currants in the middle of a round, then add a very small piece of butter and a sprinkling of sugar. Brush the outer edge of the pastry with the egg, then gather the pastry rim together in the centre and pinch to seal the filling. Turn the cake over, then roll it gently with a rolling pin, just until the cake is slightly flattened. Continue with the other rounds of pastry until all the ingredients are used up.

4 Place the cakes on a baking sheet and brush with more egg. Sprinkle with sugar, make a cut in the top of each cake and decorate with candied peel. Bake for about 10 minutes, or until the pastry is golden brown. Remove the Eccles cakes from the oven, allow them to cool slightly and serve warm.

One of the happiest culinary marriages is between chocolate and pear, and it's one of my favourite combinations, too, so you can imagine how much I adore this cake. It's amazing, to say the least! The pear keeps the cake moist while the chocolate lends a lovely taste and texture contrast. The surprise ingredient is the burnt butter, which provides a smoky nuttiness.

Bittersweet Chocolate Pear Cake

PREP
15–25 minutes
COOKING
40–50 minutes
SERVES 8

115g (4oz) butter, plus extra for greasing
100g (3½oz) plain flour, plus extra for dusting
1 tbsp baking powder
3 free-range eggs
175g (6oz) caster sugar
4 small pears, diced, plus 1 small pear, sliced, to decorate
175g (6oz) dark chocolate, broken into pieces, plus extra, grated, to decorate
100ml (3½fl oz) crème fraîche, to decorate

1 Preheat the oven to 180°C/fan 160°C/gas mark 4.

2 Butter and flour a 23cm (9in) springform cake tin. In a small bowl, sift together the flour and baking powder. Set aside. In a large bowl, whisk the eggs with an electric whisk until they are pale and very thick. Set aside.

3 Heat the butter over a medium heat in a medium-sized saucepan, until browned. As it cooks, it will foam up. Stir occasionally and scrape the solids off the bottom of the pan as they accumulate. (The butter goes from browned to burnt in less than a minute, so watch it closely.) When browned, remove from the heat and pour into a separate bowl. Set aside.

4 Add the sugar to the eggs and whisk for a few more minutes.

5 When the eggs start to lose their volume, change the speed on the whisk to low and add one-third of the flour mixture, then half the melted butter, one-third of the flour, the remainder of the butter and the remainder of the flour. Mix until barely combined to avoid losing more volume.

6 Pour the batter into the prepared tin and arrange the diced pears and dark chocolate on top. Bake for 40–50 minutes or until the cake is a light golden brown colour. Test the cake by inserting a toothpick into the centre of the cake – if it comes out clean, the cake is ready.

7 Let the cake cool in the tin for 10 minutes, then transfer to a cooling rack. Serve each slice warm, decorated with a teaspoonful of crème fraîche, a pear slice and some grated dark chocolate.

At all momentous occasions I would expect every guest to have something to take home with them to eat the next day. So this is my New Year's version. Using festive flavours that are light after an indulgent evening, this bundt is not only show-stopping to look at, but delicious, too.

CLEMENTINE & COINTREAU SYRUP BUNDT CAKE

PREP
20 minutes,
plus cooling
COOKING
1 hour –1 hour 20 minutes
SERVES 16

For the sponge

360g (12½oz) unsalted butter, softened, plus extra for greasing

450g (1lb) caster sugar

6 large free-range eggs, lightly beaten

grated rind of 6 clementines

500g (1lb 2oz) self-raising flour, plus extra for dusting

8 tbsp clementine juice

edible gold lustre spray (available online, optional)

For the syrup

thin strips of rind (no pith) from 1 clementine

8 tbsp clementine juice

200g (7oz) icing sugar

75ml (2½fl oz) orange liqueur

1 Preheat oven to 180°C/fan 160°C/gas mark 4. Grease a large cathedral bundt cake mould (I used one that was 21cm/8¼in in diameter and 10cm/4in deep), lightly dust it with flour and set it aside.

2 Cream the butter and sugar together with a wooden spoon or an electric whisk until light and fluffy, then slowly add the eggs and clementine rind, beating well after each addition. Fold in the flour, then the clementine juice, and spoon the mixture into the tin.

3 Bake for 1 hour–1 hour 20 minutes until a skewer inserted into the centre comes out with just a few moist crumbs stuck to it. You may need to cover it after about 45 minutes

to stop it browning too much. Set it on a wire rack to cool for 15 minutes, then turn out the cake and prick it all over with a cocktail stick or skewer.

4 While the cake is cooling, make the syrup. Place the strips of clementine rind and juice in a saucepan with the icing sugar and heat gently until the sugar has completely dissolved.

5 Boil the syrup for another 2–3 minutes, then remove from the heat and strain out the rind. Finally, add the orange liqueur. Spoon the syrup evenly over the cake. Leave the bundt to sit until the syrup has been absorbed, then spray it with edible gold lustre, if using, to give it a shimmery finish.

YOUR FAVOURITE CAKE RECIPES

Now is the time to ask the generation (or two or three!) above you what their favourite cake recipes are and capture your family cake story!

YOUR Favourite CaKe RecipeS

This pudding is so quick to make that sometimes I feel I should apologize to my guests for spending so little time on it. It tastes wonderful, too, especially with the addition of the spiced walnuts (you will have leftovers from the recipe, but it's no hardship as they make very moreish nibbles). I really like the contrast between the crunch and spiciness of the walnuts and the creamy texture of the posset. I hope you do, too.

ORANGE POSSETS WITH SPICED WALNUTS

For the orange possets

2 × 284ml cartons double cream

100g (3½oz) caster sugar

100ml (3½fl oz) orange juice

50ml (2fl oz) lemon juice

2 tbsp orange liqueur (optional)

For the spiced walnuts

1 tbsp honey

2 tsp olive oil

200g (7oz) walnut halves

½ tsp coarse salt

2 tbsp sugar

1 tsp ground cumin

½ tsp ground allspice

½ tsp ground cinnamon

⅛ tsp cayenne pepper

PREP
25 minutes,
plus chilling
COOKING
10 minutes
SERVES 4

1 To make the possets, gently heat the cream and sugar in a small pan. Stir constantly until the sugar has dissolved, then heat until almost boiling. Cook gently for about 3 minutes, stirring all the time – be careful not to let it boil over.

2 Remove from the heat and stir in the fruit juices, then add the liqueur, if using. Leave to cool for 5 minutes (this is especially important if you're using delicate glasses to serve). Pour into serving dishes and chill in the refrigerator for at least 4 hours, until ready to use.

3 For the spiced walnuts, line a large baking sheet with foil. Heat the honey, olive oil and

1 tablespoon cold water in a large nonstick frying pan over a medium heat, until fully combined. Add the walnuts and toss to coat.

4 Sprinkle the salt, sugar, cumin, allspice, cinnamon and cayenne pepper over the nuts and stir until fully coated. Cook over a medium heat for a further 4–5 minutes, stirring continuously, until the nuts are slightly browned.

5 Transfer the nuts to the prepared baking sheet and spread to form a single layer. Allow to cool completely before using. Place 2 or 3 walnuts on top of each posset. Store the remaining walnuts in an airtight container.

A good meringue is crisp on the outside and chewy on the inside. Meringues are simple to make when you know how: the trick is to cook them slowly at a low temperature. Sandwich them around a dollop of whipped cream, then drizzle over some chocolate sauce and you have an instant dessert. They taste equally good crushed with a mixture of cream and Greek yogurt with fresh fruit. You can keep them in an airtight tin for up to two weeks, or store them in the freezer for a standby pudding.

CANDY-STRIPED MERINGUES

PREP
40 minutes
COOKING
40 minutes
MAKES 30

4 free-range egg whites
225g (8oz) icing sugar, sifted
3 drops of vanilla extract
few drops each of black and red food colouring

1 Preheat the oven to 140°C/fan 120°C/gas mark 1 and line a couple of baking sheets with nonstick baking paper.

2 Whisk the egg whites and icing sugar until the mixture is thick and forms firm peaks. Add the vanilla extract and whisk for a further 2 minutes.

3 Using a small paintbrush, straw or the handle of a spoon, paint 2 or 3 stripes of black food colouring on the inside of a piping bag.

4 Fit the piping bag with a star-shaped nozzle and spoon half the meringue mixture into the bag. Pipe small 2cm (¾in) high star shapes onto the prepared baking sheets. Repeat steps 3 and 4 with red food colouring and the remaining meringue mixture.

5 Bake the meringues for 40 minutes, until they are crisp but not brown. Turn off the oven and leave the meringues to cool inside overnight, with the oven door slightly ajar, to ensure that the outsides are crispy and the insides are soft and chewy.

These are so pretty that whenever I serve them I'm greeted by ooohs and aaahs, and people often tell me that they don't have the heart to eat them. But they would be missing out on a treat, as these silky milky delights are lightly scented with rose essence and taste as good as they look.

Rose Pannacotta

PREP
25–30 minutes,
plus chilling
COOKING
10 minutes
SERVES 6

6 tsp powdered gelatine
350ml (12fl oz) milk
700ml (1¼ pints) double cream
950g (2lb 2oz) caster sugar
½ tsp rose-petal essence
6 edible rose transfers (available online)

1 Put 6 tablespoons cold water in a small heatproof bowl, then sprinkle the gelatine over the top. Leave to soak for 5 minutes, then set the bowl over a small saucepan of simmering water for 5 minutes or until a clear liquid forms. Set aside.

2 Place the milk, cream and sugar in a large saucepan and heat, stirring constantly. When at boiling point, remove from the heat, add the rose-petal essence and gelatine liquid, and stir. Divide this mixture between 6 dariole moulds, ramekin dishes or teacups and refrigerate for about 3 hours until firmly set (the mixture shouldn't sag when you tilt the mould).

3 Run the tip of a small pointed knife around the top edge of the moulds to loosen them. Next, fill a large bowl with hot water and dip the moulds into the water just to the rim for about 10 seconds. Place a plate on top of each mould and, keeping it firmly in place, invert the plate and the mould at the same time. Give the mould a shake, still holding the plate in place underneath it, then lift the mould off carefully. If the pannacotta doesn't release easily, dip the mould in water again.

4 Before serving, apply a rose transfer to the top of each pannacotta, holding each transfer in place for at least 30 seconds and delicately rubbing the reverse side to ensure that the image transfers.

The pleasure of receiving a gift that has been handmade with love and care outweighs that of receiving a shop-bought present any day. People's time is priceless and giving a delicious gift such as this one gives the impression that you have spent a good amount of time slaving away to achieve taste and perfection.

engraved EARL GREY TRUFFLE HEARTS

PREP
10 minutes,
plus chilling
MAKES
about 25

125g (4½oz) chocolate
(I use half dark and half milk)

100g (3½oz) extra-thick cream

2 tsp loose Earl Grey tea

1 Cut the chocolate into pieces that are as small as you can make them. Place them in a bowl ready for the hot cream to be poured onto them.

2 Heat the cream and the tea leaves in a pan over a low heat to infuse the flavour. When the mixture starts to boil, remove from the heat and pour through a strainer onto the chocolate.

3 Leave for a couple of minutes to ensure the chocolate has melted, then mix into a silky consistency (this mixture is called a ganache). Line a baking sheet with nonstick baking paper, then pour the ganache onto it. I start in the middle and spread the mixture with a spatula, trying for an even coverage of around 15mm (⅝ in) thickness.

4 Pop the ganache into the refrigerator for a couple of hours until set. Now use a shape cutter to create your truffles – you can buy a huge variety on the trusty internet or in good cookshops. I also stamp the truffles with an unused ink-stamp to mark friends' names and the dates of events – a personal touch that helps make a tea party extra memorable.

These love spoons are the grown-up version of a lollipop, and each time I make them I vary the flavours slightly to keep them interesting. So my man never knows exactly what he's putting in his mouth!

CHOCOLATE-COVERED love SPOONS

PREP
15 minutes,
plus chilling
COOKING
5 minutes
MAKES 4

75g (3oz) dark chocolate
1 tbsp brandy
pinch of chilli powder
¼ tsp ground cinnamon
pinch of ground nutmeg

1 Break the chocolate into pieces and melt it in a heatproof bowl set over a saucepan of barely simmering water, ensuring the base of the bowl doesn't touch the water below. Reserve 3 tablespoons of melted chocolate in a separate bowl for coating.

2 Combine the brandy and spices with the melted chocolate. Fill the bowls of 4 ornate spoons with the melted chocolate mixture, then set them on a tray and place them in the refrigerator for 10 minutes to allow the chocolate to harden a little.

3 Remove the spoons from the refrigerator and coat them with the remaining melted chocolate. Allow to chill once more until hard.

4 Serve the spoons with hot after-dinner drinks.

Mmm! There's nothing more decadent than having a tray of luscious juicy oysters to feast on. The runny salty juices and the soft tender bite of the oyster with its briny, tangy flavours – it's an all-time favourite of mine. I also live in hope that maybe one day I might find a pearl in one of these beauties. To add a bit more glitz and glamour to this luxurious treat, why not sprinkle on some real gold? You might not be able to taste it, but it sure makes the dish look spectacular.

24-CaRaT OYSTeRS

PREP
15 minutes
SERVES 6

12 oysters

1 tsp cayenne pepper

1 sheet of edible gold leaf (available from most good cake shops or the internet)

plenty of rock salt

12 lemon wedges

1 To open an oyster, hold it down firmly with a tea towel and, using an oyster knife, prise it open at the hinge, twisting if you need to. When it opens, slide the knife between the two shell halves and work your way round, easing them apart. Remove the 'lid', being careful not to lose any of the juices.

2 Now slide the knife underneath the oyster so that it is completely separated from the shell (but still sitting in it) and will slip out easily when tipped into the mouth.

3 Sprinkle a pinch of cayenne pepper over each oyster in the shell.

4 To make gold flakes, use tweezers to break off tiny pieces from the gold leaf sheet and put them in a small bowl. Sprinkle 4–6 flakes over each oyster.

5 Arrange the oysters in their shells on a cake stand or serving dish. (If you cover the plate with rock salt first, it will stop the oysters sliding around.) Serve each oyster with a wedge of lemon for squeezing over.

6 To eat, hold the shell with the shallower end towards you. Tip the shell back so that the oyster slides directly into your mouth.

When my grandmother made chopped liver, the rest of the family would vigorously fight over who got to take the leftovers home. This recipe is a little more refined, but it's a great crowd-pleaser and always one of the first platters at my parties to be polished off. The guests love the pairing of silky smooth parfait with crispy filo pastry. The little baskets look stunning, too.

CHICKEN LIVER PARFAIT
IN a FILO PASTRY basket

PREP
40 minutes
COOKING
12–15 minutes
MAKES 24

175g (6oz) butter
1kg (2lb 4oz) chicken livers, cleaned
50ml (2fl oz) brandy
4 tbsp double cream
salt and black pepper
8 sheets of ready-rolled filo pastry
24 pearl onions

1 Preheat the oven to 220°C/fan 200°C/gas mark 7. Heat 50g (1¾oz) of the butter in a frying pan until very hot. Add the chicken livers and cook for 3–4 minutes, turning occasionally so they cook evenly but are still pink in the middle. Add the brandy and cook until the alcohol has evaporated. Take off the heat and allow the livers to cool slightly. In a clean pan, melt another 50g (1¾oz) of the butter, then blend it with the chicken livers in a food processor. Add the cream and blend to incorporate. Season with salt and pepper and set aside.

2 Melt the remaining butter. Using a pastry brush, brush one side of the first sheet of pastry with butter, then top with a second sheet. Butter this sheet and top with a third. Butter this and finish with a fourth (butter this too). Cut out 12 layered pastry circles using an 8cm (3¼in) pastry cutter and press these into a 12-hole mini-muffin pan. Repeat with the remaining 4 sheets of pastry. Bake for 6 minutes, or until golden.

3 Remove from the pan and cool on a wire rack. Transfer the parfait to a piping bag fitted with a star-shaped nozzle and pipe into the baskets. Decorate each with a pearl onion.

If you like 'The Addams Family', you'll love this. Sometimes I hide toy coffins at the bottom of the couscous! Beyond the visuals, though, it's a really healthy dish. Buy seasonal vegetables and make your own dipping sauces such as peppered houmous, aubergine or mackerel mousse, or tzatziki. Weird and fabulous!

SALAD CEMETERY

2 tsp squid ink (available from good fishmongers) or 1 tsp black food colouring

200ml (7fl oz) just-boiled water

150g (5½oz) couscous

1 tsp olive oil

salt and black pepper

assorted micro herbs (available from large supermarkets), such as red radish, rocket, mizuna, mustard and cress, coriander and pea shoots

assorted miniature vegetables (available from large supermarkets), such as baby courgettes, radishes, young fennel, baby carrots, baby pak choi – 150g (5½oz) per type of vegetable used

selection of dips, such as houmous or tzatziki, to serve

1 Mix the ink or food colouring with the water in a measuring jug, then pour this over the couscous in a large bowl. Add the oil and season to taste with salt and pepper. Cover the bowl with clingfilm and set aside for about 10 minutes until all the liquid is absorbed and the couscous has puffed up. Fluff up the grains with a fork.

2 Transfer the coloured couscous to a serving dish and arrange the herbs and vegetables on top, poking these into the couscous as if you were planting a miniature garden.

3 Serve with a selection of dips, giving each guest a small pair of scissors to allow them to trim their own micro herbs.

YOUR FAVOURITE SHOW-OFF RECIPES

YOUR FAVOURITE SHOW-OFF RECIPES

I remember the feelings I had on entering a fudge shop for the first time as if it were yesterday. It was like Fudge Narnia! I was at a theme park (where you lose your sense with money!) and I was overwhelmed by the array of choices and the quantities on offer. They sold every flavour of fudge imaginable and some that I'd never even heard of, and I had the freedom to choose whatever I liked. I asked for countless different types but, disappointingly, many of them tasted similar – except for rum & raisin. This flavour has remained a firm favourite of mine to this day.

RUM & RAISIN FUDGE

PREP
10 minutes

TOTAL TIME
40 minutes, plus
3 hours for setting

MAKES
24 squares

50ml (2fl oz) dark rum

100g (3½oz) raisins, roughly chopped

100g (3½oz) butter, plus extra for greasing

397g can sweetened condensed milk

125ml (4fl oz) milk

450g (1lb) demerara sugar

1 Put the dark rum in a bowl and add the chopped raisins. Set aside to soak.

2 Grease a 20cm (8in) square cake tin and line it with nonstick baking paper.

3 Combine the remaining ingredients in a large nonstick saucepan over a medium heat and stir until the sugar dissolves.

4 Remove the sugar crystals. Once the solution starts to boil, put a lid on the pan and keep it in place for 3 minutes. Take off the lid and remove any stubborn crystals by wiping the inside of the pan with a pastry brush dipped in warm water.

5 Bring the mixture to the boil, then simmer gently for 10–15 minutes, stirring constantly, until it reaches 116°C (240°F).

6 Remove the saucepan from the heat and allow the temperature of the mixture to drop to 110°C (230°F) before beating it. Beat with a wooden spoon for 10 minutes until the mixture is very thick and almost has the consistency and look of smooth peanut butter. This step is vital for thickening the fudge, so ensure you beat the mixture until it is very thick and stiff.

7 Stir in the raisins and the rum, then pour the mixture into the prepared tin and set aside for about 3 hours to cool.

8 When the fudge is completely cold, cut it into 24 small squares using a sharp knife.

Every Christmas, from the age of five to at least my early teens, I'd make floral creams with my gran to give as gifts. I remember being impressed at how easy it was to create something so yummy and elegant. The mint creams are great at the end of a tea party and I'm a huge fan of the rose-scented creams, too.

Floral Creams

PREP
25 minutes,
plus chilling
MAKES 20

45ml (1½fl oz) double cream

1 drop of food colouring of your choice

45ml (1½fl oz) rose, violet, mint or lavender syrup (available online)

275g (9oz) icing sugar, plus extra for dusting

100g (3½oz) dark chocolate, broken into pieces

1 tsp sunflower oil

20 edible sugared rose or violet petals, sugared mint leaf pieces or lavender florets, to decorate (available online)

1 Place the cream, food colouring and syrup in a bowl and mix well. Sift the icing sugar over the cream mixture and stir to combine.

2 Dust a work surface lightly with icing sugar, then tip the cream mixture out onto it and knead with your hands until it comes together in a firm ball. Wrap in clingfilm and place in the refrigerator for about 30 minutes. Remove the fondant from the refrigerator and unwrap it. Divide it into 20 teaspoon-sized lumps, roll them into balls and place on a plate. Set aside.

3 Melt the chocolate in a bowl set over a saucepan of simmering water, ensuring the base of the bowl does not touch the water. Stir in the sunflower oil, then remove the chocolate from the heat. Allow to cool for about 10 minutes.

4 Meanwhile, line a 39 × 35cm (15½ × 14in) baking sheet with nonstick baking paper. Working quickly, dip the fondant balls halfway into the melted chocolate one at a time. Place each coated ball carefully onto the nonstick baking paper. Top each with an edible sugared petal or leaf and set aside to harden in the refrigerator for 15 minutes. Serve as they are, or in individual petit-four cases, if you wish.

I was quite shocked, when researching this recipe, to discover that cola cubes are not actually made using cola! I had to tell my brother, as this was always his favourite sweet when we were growing up (they often filled his pockets) and, as a consequence, I always think of cola cubes as a bit of a boys' sweet. I would feel quite grown up and privileged when my big brother allowed me to have one! Images of him in the 1980s playing with a Rubik's Cube in the garden, shoving red sugary cubes into his mouth, will always remain a vivid childhood memory.

Cola Cubes

PREP
15 minutes

TOTAL TIME
1¼ hours, plus 1–2 hours for setting,

MAKES 40

nonstick baking spray, for greasing (optional)

450g (1lb) granulated sugar

½ tsp cream of tartar

1 tbsp liquid glucose

½ tsp vanilla extract

½ tsp lemon extract

½ tsp orange extract

¼ tsp cinnamon extract

½ tsp citric acid

about 5 drops of red food colouring

icing sugar, to coat

1 Prepare your sweet moulds. You will need more than 1 mould for the quantity given, or you can work in batches. Either use silicone ice-cube trays sprayed with nonstick baking spray or, if you are feeling adventurous, make your own.

2 Put the sugar, 150ml (¼ pint) cold water, cream of tartar and liquid glucose into a saucepan over a low heat and heat it until the sugar has dissolved, stirring slowly.

3 When the mixture comes to the boil, remove the sugar crystals that are stuck to the inside of the pan above the bubbling solution (*see* page 90, step 4).

4 Keep the mixture bubbling, without stirring, until it reaches 154°C (310°F). Take the pan off the heat and allow the mixture to cool to approximately 110°C (230°F), then stir in the flavourings, citric acid and colouring.

5 Fill the sweet moulds with the mixture using a piston funnel, a Pyrex jug or a spoon – but be wary of drips. Leave for 1–2 hours until completely cool.

6 Pop the sweets out of the ice cube trays as you would ice cubes. If taking them out of an icing sugar mould, simply pick them out. Roll the cubes in icing sugar (to stop them from sticking to one another) and store them in an airtight container.

I'd never tasted homemade marshmallows until my later years. Making them from scratch allows you to flavour them with anything you want – in that way you can transform the humble marshmallow into something quite indulgent and suitable for grown-ups.

Marshmallows

PREP
20 minutes

TOTAL TIME
50 minutes,
plus 4 hours for
setting

MAKES 24

butter or nonstick spray, for greasing
300–400g (10–14oz) icing sugar
225ml (7½fl oz) cold water
20g (¾oz) powdered gelatine
400g (14oz) granulated sugar
240ml (8fl oz) golden syrup
¼ tsp salt
2 tsp mint extract (or use 2 tsp vanilla extract, ½ tsp almond extract or 2 tsp lemon or orange extract)

1 Lightly grease the base of a 33 × 23 × 5cm (13 × 9 × 2in) baking tray. Line the base of the tray with nonstick silicone baking paper, then sift about 3 tbsp of the icing sugar onto the base.

2 Put half the cold water into the bowl of a food mixer and sprinkle over the gelatine. Don't switch on the motor just yet!

3 Put the granulated sugar, golden syrup, salt and the remaining cold water into a saucepan. Stir over a medium heat until the sugar dissolves and the mixture comes to the boil. When it does, remove the sugar crystals that are stuck to the inside of the pan (*see* page 90, step 4). Increase the heat and boil, without stirring, until the syrup reaches 116°C (240°F). Remove from the heat.

4 Run your food mixer on a low speed as you slowly pour the hot syrup into the gelatine mixture in a thin stream down the side of the bowl. Once it's all in, gradually increase the speed to high and beat for at least 10 minutes. The mixture will triple in volume. Add the flavouring and beat for another minute.

5 Scrape or pour the marshmallow mixture onto the prepared baking sheet and spread it using a damp spatula. Then sift 3–4 tablespoons icing sugar over the mallow and leave to stand, uncovered, at room temperature for about 4 hours until set.

6 Remove the marshmallow from the baking sheet by running a small sharp knife around the edge to loosen it. Turn it out onto a surface dusted with lots more sifted icing sugar. Peel off the silicone paper and cover the top with plenty more sifted icing sugar.

7 Cut the marshmallow into 20 squares using kitchen scissors, a pizza cutter or a sharp knife. Dip the cut sides in additional icing sugar. Shake off any excess sugar and store the marshmallows in an airtight container at room temperature.

If you ever attend a party of mine, you'll realize that I'm a fan of rose. I may offer you rose tea, rose cocktail or even rose sandwiches! So it's no surprise that Turkish delight – with its sweet rose-flavoured jelly – holds a special place in my childhood memories. But it wasn't until I was around 10 years old that I tasted the traditional (real) deal, which came in a variety of flavours – nut, date, orange and, of course, rose! I love this gooey orange and pistachio combination.

TURKISH DELIGHT

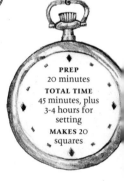

butter, for greasing

icing sugar, for dusting

600g (1lb 5oz) caster sugar

3 tbsp golden syrup

125ml (4fl oz) orange juice

3 tbsp grated orange rind (about 4 large oranges)

20g (¾oz) powdered gelatine

100g (3½oz) cornflour

flavouring (1 tbsp vanilla extract, 1½ tsp rose water or ½ tsp mint extract)

5–8 drops of red food colouring

100g (3½oz) pistachio nuts, chopped (optional)

PREP
20 minutes

TOTAL TIME
45 minutes, plus 3-4 hours for setting

MAKES 20 squares

1 Grease a 20cm (8in) square cake tin with butter and line it with nonstick silicone baking paper. Give the lining a generous sprinkling of sifted icing sugar.

2 Put 350ml (12fl oz) cold water, the caster sugar and golden syrup in a large saucepan and bring to the boil over a medium–high heat. When the mixture comes to the boil, remove the sugar crystals that are stuck to the inside of the pan (see page 90, step 4). Continue to boil the mixture, without stirring, until it reaches 116°C (240°F).

3 Meanwhile, stir together the orange juice and rind in a jug or small bowl, sprinkle over the gelatine, stir again, then set aside.

4 In a small bowl, dissolve the cornflour in 125ml (4½fl oz) cold water. When the sugar mixture has reached a temperature of 116°C

(240°F), stir in the cornflour mix. Put the pan over a medium–low heat and simmer, stirring gently, until the mixture is very thick – this will take only a couple of minutes.

5 Remove the pan from the heat and stir in the orange juice mixture, the flavouring of your choice, the food colouring and the pistachios, if liked. Pour the Turkish delight mixture into the prepared tin and leave to set in a cool, dry place (not in the refrigerator) for 3–4 hours. When cool, sprinkle the top with a thick layer of sifted icing sugar. Cut into 20 cubes and roll them in sifted icing sugar. Knock off any excess sugar, then pack away in an airtight container and store at room temperature. Alternatively, hide it away in a homemade Secret Hollow Book (see page 100).

How to Make a
Secret Hollow book

When my granny bought me my first box of Turkish delight, I remember being wooed by the jewel-like box that it came in. The presentation of gifts is everything! By taking the time to track down a beautiful old book (which cost pennies in second-hand shops) you can turn it into a Secret Hollow Book and create a gift that someone special can treasure forever.

YOU WILL NEED

newspaper ✂ PVA glue and container to mix it in ✂ beautiful hardback vintage book (you can pick one up cheaply in junk shops, charity shops or at car boot sales) ✂ small paintbrush ✂ £1 coin (to use as a spacer) ✂ metal ruler ✂ pencil ✂ sharp scalpel or craft knife ✂ clear varnish (optional)

1 Lay out a few sheets of newspaper to protect your work surface, then mix up a glue solution of PVA and water in a 50:50 ratio.

2 Flick past the book's title pages to the first page of full text – this will be your first cut-out page. Turn this page over, too. You will cut this page last (this will make sense later on!). Hold the bulk of the book together and brush the outside edges with the glue solution. Use enough to stick them together – you may need two coats.

3 Put the £1 coin into the book on top of the first glued page and below the unglued pages. Close the book and allow it to dry. Once it is dry, remove the coin and stick the back cover to the glued pages and allow to dry again.

4 Open your book to the first glued page and, using a metal ruler, draw a rectangular border 2.5cm (1in) from the edges of the page. Carefully and slowly cut along the lines using the scalpel or craft knife, resting the blade against the metal ruler as you cut. Keep the blade vertical or the hole will slope as you cut deeper into the book. Continue cutting until you are on the last page.

5 Remove the cut-out paper, then brush the inside of the cut-out hollow with PVA solution, then brush glue on the top of the first glued page. Now turn over the first loose page onto the glue, this will stick it to the glued and cut-out section of the book. Close the book and leave to dry thoroughly.

6 Open the book to the first page before the cut-out section, which is now glued to the cut-out section. Carefully cut out the shape of the rectangle of the hollow beneath this page using the scalpel or craft knife, covering your earlier pencil markings and creating a neat finish on your top page. As an optional extra, you can now brush the entire inside of the hollow with a coat of clear varnish, so that you can wipe it clean after storing sweeties inside! And then you're done and ready to fill your hollow book with secret sweet treats.

There are some flavour combinations that you need to test to validate the hype. Rose and cucumber is one of them. I'm not sure why this cocktail is so delicious. I can only presume that it's down to the combined sweetness of the rose, the sharpness of the gin and the freshness of the cucumber.

ENGLISH DELIGHT

6 fine slices of cucumber

45ml (1½fl oz) Hendrick's gin

30ml (1fl oz) crème de rose or rose syrup

ice cubes

125ml (4fl oz) lemonade

PREP
10 minutes

TOTAL TIME
10 minutes

MAKES 2

1 For the cucumber 'flower' garnish, place 2 slices of cucumber flat on top of one another, with the smallest of them on the top. Fold the third slice in half, then in quarters, so it resembles a flower and has a triangle shape. Place the first 2 slices in the bottom of a glass then place the folded one on top. Repeat for the second glass.

2 Mix the gin, crème de rose or rose syrup and ice in a cocktail shaker. Pour the cocktail into the glasses, on top of the garnish.

3 Top up with lemonade and serve immediately.

How to Make

Treat Boxes

Receiving or giving – I'm not sure which I prefer! Many of the recipes in this book cost as little as a bag of sugar to make, but the effort taken to make them is the thing that provides the pleasure – along with the contents, of course! Keeping with this 'made from love' theme, these handmade boxes are incredibly simple to assemble and look fabulous as a gift, end-of-party treat or even at a wedding.

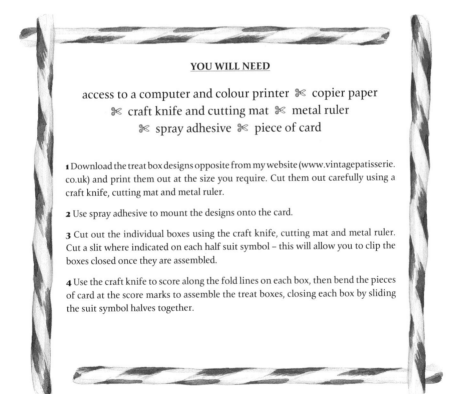

YOU WILL NEED

access to a computer and colour printer ✂ copier paper ✂ craft knife and cutting mat ✂ metal ruler ✂ spray adhesive ✂ piece of card

1 Download the treat box designs opposite from my website (www.vintagepatisserie.co.uk) and print them out at the size you require. Cut them out carefully using a craft knife, cutting mat and metal ruler.

2 Use spray adhesive to mount the designs onto the card.

3 Cut out the individual boxes using the craft knife, cutting mat and metal ruler. Cut a slit where indicated on each half suit symbol – this will allow you to clip the boxes closed once they are assembled.

4 Use the craft knife to score along the fold lines on each box, then bend the pieces of card at the score marks to assemble the treat boxes, closing each box by sliding the suit symbol halves together.

I was never a fan of liquorice as a child. This stuck with me for years until I tried a toffee liquorice that was subtly scented with anise and had the smooth, creamy texture and mellow flavour of caramel. Gone was the 'break your teeth, dye your tongue black' liquorice square I remember! The version below encourages you to play around with cutting shapes and stamping letters for that personal touch. And you can double the amount of anise extract for a stronger liquorice flavour, if that's what you like.

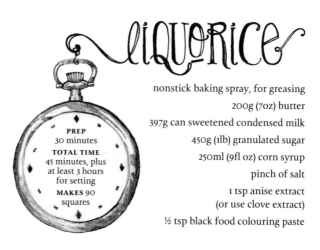

liquorice

PREP
30 minutes

TOTAL TIME
45 minutes, plus
at least 3 hours
for setting

MAKES 90
squares

nonstick baking spray, for greasing
200g (7oz) butter
397g can sweetened condensed milk
450g (1lb) granulated sugar
250ml (9fl oz) corn syrup
pinch of salt
1 tsp anise extract
(or use clove extract)
½ tsp black food colouring paste

1 Line a 23cm (9in) square cake tin with kitchen foil and then spray with nonstick baking spray.

2 In quite a large saucepan, melt the butter over a medium heat. Once melted, add the condensed milk, sugar, corn syrup and salt, and stir until combined.

3 Bring the mixture to the boil, stirring constantly. The mixture will darken as it heats up and you'll see some dark brown bits in it, but these won't affect the final product. Once it comes to the boil, continue to stir constantly to prevent it burning on the base of the pan. Attach a sugar thermometer and boil the mixture until it reaches 121ºC (250ºF).

4 Remove the mixture from the heat and stir in the anise extract and food colouring, mixing until thoroughly combined.

5 Pour the liquorice into the prepared cake tin. Allow it to set at room temperature – this could take anywhere from about 3 hours to overnight. Pop it into the refrigerator to speed up the process.

6 Cut the liquorice into 90 2.5cm (1in) squares using kitchen scissors. Alternatively, cut out different shapes and emboss them with a stamp so that they resemble Pontefract cakes. Wrap individual sweets in waxed paper or clingfilm to store.

Gumdrops won a place in my sweetie book due to their versatility. Sweet, chewy and full of flavour, they can be shaped in any mould. When I was very young, my mum would always allow us to put one in the centre of her freshly baked fairy cakes!

GUMDROPS

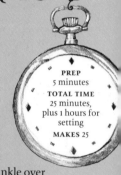

PREP
5 minutes

TOTAL TIME
25 minutes,
plus 1 hours for
setting

MAKES 25

20g (¾oz) powdered gelatine

300g (10oz) granulated sugar

¼ tsp citric acid

½ tsp flavouring (try lime, lemon, almond or cinnamon)

3–5 drops of food colouring (try green, yellow, red or blue)

nonstick baking spray, for greasing

1 Pour 200ml (7fl oz) cold water into a small bowl and sprinkle over the powdered gelatine.

2 In a saucepan, combine another 200ml (7fl oz) cold water with 250g (9oz) of the sugar. Stir to dissolve the sugar and bring the mixture to the boil. Boil until the temperature on a sugar thermometer reads 130°C (266°F). Remove the saucepan from the heat and whisk in the citric acid and the gelatine mixture until fully dissolved.

3 If you would like to make gumdrops of different colours and flavours, separate the mixture into the required number of different bowls at this stage. Mix in the flavourings and colourings of your choice, then pour each batch of the mixture into silicone gumdrop moulds in the shape and size of your choice, sprayed with nonstick baking spray. If you have more than one batch of colours and flavours, once the first batch is moulded, reheat the next batch over a very low heat to pour it into the moulds. Leave to set, either at room temperature or in the refrigerator, for at least 1 hour.

4 Remove the sweets from the moulds and roll the gumdrops in the remaining sugar to coat. Store in an airtight container.

YOUR FAVOURITE SWEET TREATS

YOUR FAVOURITE SWEET TREATS

G&TEA
ANYONE?

There are many tales about the invention of the Gimlet, but most include a 'Dr Gimlet' a 'Sailor' and a mention of the fact that this sweet-and-sour drink was invented as a cure for something. Hmm...

BASIC GIMLET

PREP
1 min
SERVES 1

50ml (2fl oz) gin
30ml (1fl oz) lime cordial
ice cubes

1 Mix the ingredients in a shaker and serve!

Serving delicious drinks at large parties is a hard task without a full bar of mixologists, right? NO! Let me introduce Mr Punch. He is a big bowl of cocktail normally containing fruit, alcohol and a mixer. Of course, I like to use British flavours, but you can tailor this to your taste. My biggest tips: use lemon to preserve freshness and use homemade mixers such as cold tea to keep costs down. All that's left is to hold your teacup up and make a toast to all those present, to your loved ones and, of course, to THE QUEEN!

PiMM'S iCeD Tea

SERVES 1

PREP 5 mins, plus chilling

ice cubes

90ml (3¼fl oz) Pimm's No. 1

180ml (6¼fl oz) brewed orange pekoe tea, chilled

1½ tsp agave syrup or honey

1½ tbsp freshly squeezed lemon juice

citrus wedges, mint sprigs, quartered strawberries and cucumber ribbons, to garnish

1 Fill a highball glass with ice. Add the Pimm's, tea, agave syrup or honey and lemon juice and stir well. Decorate the drink lavishly.

THYMe PUNCH

SERVES 6

5 tsp caster sugar

35ml (1¼fl oz) freshly squeezed lemon juice

250ml (9fl oz) Hendrick's gin

leaves from 6 sprigs of thyme, very roughly chopped, plus extra to decorate

650ml (1⅛ pints) cloudy lemonade

ice cubes

1 Pour the sugar into a jug. Add the lemon juice and gin, followed by the thyme. Top up with lemonade, stir and chill.

2 Just before serving, add a handful of ice cubes and stir again. Decorate the punch with extra thyme.

MeMORabLe BRiTiSH STReeT PaRTieS

In western folklore, Bloody Mary was a witch. It was believed that if you stood in front of a mirror and said her name three times she would appear in the mirror. We can thank her for numerous films, computer games, TV programmes and the infamous drink. So let's raise our glasses to Mary: Thank you Bloody Mary, thank you Bloody Mary, thank you Bloody Mary!

BLOODY MARY SHOTS

PREP
20 minutes
SERVES 6

½ shallot, roughly chopped

1 tbsp freshly grated horseradish

1½ sticks of celery, roughly chopped

200g (7oz) chopped tomatoes

¼ tsp celery salt, plus an extra 2 tbsp to decorate the glasses

1½ tbsp Worcestershire sauce

½–1 tsp Tabasco sauce

¼ tsp black pepper

juice of ½ lemon (reserve the unjuiced half for wetting the glass rims)

500ml (17fl oz) tomato juice

4 tbsp vodka

1 tbsp amontillado or other dry sherry

1 Place the shallot, horseradish, 1 stick of celery, tomatoes, celery salt, Worcestershire sauce, Tabasco sauce, black pepper and lemon juice in a liquidizer and blend until smooth. Strain the mixture through a sieve, using the back of a metal spoon to push it through. Stir in the tomato juice, vodka and sherry.

2 Just before serving, wet the rim of 6 small glasses with the reserved lemon half, then turn each one upside-down and dip it in a saucer of celery salt, to coat the rim. Divide the Bloody Mary between the glasses. Trim the remaining half-stick of celery, cut it in half lengthways, then cut each length into 3 batons of equal size, using a slanted cut. Place a celery baton in each glass to serve.

In the past, I have been accused of creating drinks that are a touch on the feminine side. Of course, I disagree totally, as many male party-goers love a Lavender Pearl cocktail! But I must listen to my customers and, when I'm asked for a 'man's drink' nowadays, I offer them Gunfire. This is the kind of thing a big, strong pirate would have drunk on a cold night, so off I go to walk the plank and put the kettle on.

GUNFIRE

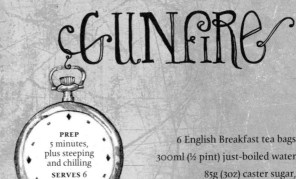

PREP
5 minutes,
plus steeping
and chilling
SERVES 6

6 English Breakfast tea bags
300ml (½ pint) just-boiled water
85g (3oz) caster sugar,
or to taste
100ml (3½fl oz) dark rum
orange rind, to decorate

1 Steep the tea bags in the water in a measuring jug for 4 minutes, adding the sugar and stirring until dissolved. Remove the tea bags. Chill the tea in the refrigerator for 30 minutes.

2 Add the rum, stir to mix, then pour into 6 teacups.

3 Decorate with orange rind and serve immediately.

While hosting a children's tea party on a very hot day, for refreshment I made some iced green-jasmine tea from the contents of my tea basket, adding berries for colour. It was an instant hit – I simply could not make it quickly enough for the children. Later, during the party, the adults cracked open a bottle of Champagne, which we added to our chilled tea – and our signature cocktail was born.

GREEN-JASMINE TEA BUBBLES

PREP
5 minutes,
plus steeping
and cooling

SERVES
5 without alcohol
and 10 with

5 green-jasmine teabags or 5 tbsp loose green-jasmine tea
200ml (7fl oz) just-boiled water
3 tbsp caster sugar, or to taste
handful of raspberries and blackberries (optional)
1 bottle of good Champagne, chilled (optional)

1 Steep the teabags or loose tea in a measuring jug in the just-boiled water for 1 minute, adding the sugar and stirring until dissolved. Remove the teabags, or strain to remove the loose tea, then add 500ml (18fl oz) cold water.

2 Taste the tea for strength, adding a touch more cold water if it's too strong, then put it in the refrigerator to chill further for 30 minutes. (If you can't wait, add a few ice cubes to speed up the chilling process.)

3 Serve in vintage teacups. For a bit of extra colour, put a couple of berries into each cup before pouring. For the alcoholic version, simply half-fill the cup with tea, then top up with an equal measure of bubbly.

My love affair with Martin(i) began in Chicago 12 years ago. Our eyes met across a crowded bar, perched high up above the city skyline. The views were extraordinary and he stole my heart, although I couldn't help but think he was a little bitter back then. But first impressions can be deceptive... Memories come flooding back when I think of the Martini cocktail, a marvellous American invention for which we must be eternally grateful. This cocktail has a personality! When I was younger, I struggled to enjoy them, but nowadays I thoroughly appreciate their bitter undertones, and enjoy experimenting with these 'Tea Tinis'.

Basic Tea Tini

PREP
10 minutes, plus steeping and chilling
SERVES 4

5 teabags of your choice

150ml (5fl oz) just-boiled water

70g (2½oz) caster sugar, or to taste

100ml (3½fl oz) vodka

30ml (1fl oz) vermouth

juice of 1 lemon

ice cubes

4 lemon wheels, to decorate

Variations

For a Flower Martini, follow the Basic Tea Tini recipe but use Lady Grey teabags, 50g (1¾oz) caster sugar, 50ml (2fl oz) dry vermouth, and add 30ml (1fl oz) elderflower liqueur. Decorate with mint sprigs.

For a Strawberry Martini, follow the Basic Tea Tini recipe but use strawberry fruit tea and decorate with strawberry halves.

1 Steep the teabags in the just-boiled water in a measuring jug for 4 minutes, adding the sugar and stirring until dissolved. Remove the teabags. Chill the tea in the refrigerator for 30 minutes.

2 Mix the vodka, vermouth and lemon juice together in a measuring jug.

3 Add the tea syrup and shake in a cocktail shaker with ice for 5–10 seconds.

4 Serve chilled in glasses decorated with lemon wheels on hatpins.

If, like me, you are a fan of violets, you will love this cocktail. Elegant in style and floral in flavour, it's a vintage delight. And if you're in the mood to show off, a decoration of delicate edible flowers is just the ticket.

PARMA VIOLET COCKTAIL

For the violet syrup

100g (3½oz) granulated sugar

¼ tsp violet flavouring

5 drops of violet colouring

For the cocktail

50ml (2fl oz) peach schnapps

50ml (2fl oz) violet syrup (*see* left)

1 tbsp lime juice

200ml (7fl oz) sparkling water

50ml (2fl oz) vodka

crushed ice

violet flowers, to decorate (optional)

PREP
45 minutes
PREP
15 minutes
MAKES 4

1 To make the violet syrup, combine 100ml (3½fl oz) cold water and the sugar in a saucepan and place the pan over a high heat. Bring to the boil, then reduce the heat and simmer for 5 minutes.

2 Take the pan off the heat and add the flavouring and colouring. Leave in the refrigerator to cool for 30 minutes.

3 When you're ready to make the cocktail, combine all the ingredients in a cocktail shaker. Strain into chilled glasses, decorated with violet flowers, if using, and serve immediately.

How to make
COCKTAIL MONKEYS

If your cocktail tastes fabulous but is lacking in visual appeal, these simple monkey cocktail pendants will give everyone that cheeky grin. Say bye bye 1980s umbrellas and hello monkey! Making them can be a little fiddly, but as long as your guests don't take them home, they can be used again and again. Try to print them on the thickest card possible before waterproofing them. We don't want Mr Monkey getting drunk!

YOU WILL NEED

access to a computer and colour printer ✂ copier paper ✂
spray adhesive ✂ thick white card ✂ paper scissors ✂
clear sticky-back plastic

1 Download the two monkey pendant designs and their mirror images opposite from my website (www.vintagepatisserie.co.uk) and print them out, then use the spray adhesive to mount your colour print-outs onto card.

2 Cut out the designs neatly, then glue the matching pairs (one front piece, one back piece) together so that the same monkey design is on both sides.

3 Cover both sides of each cocktail monkey with sticky-back plastic. Now cut out the monkeys, leaving a 1mm (1/32in) edge of plastic around each monkey to create a waterproof seal and make the pendant more long-lasting.

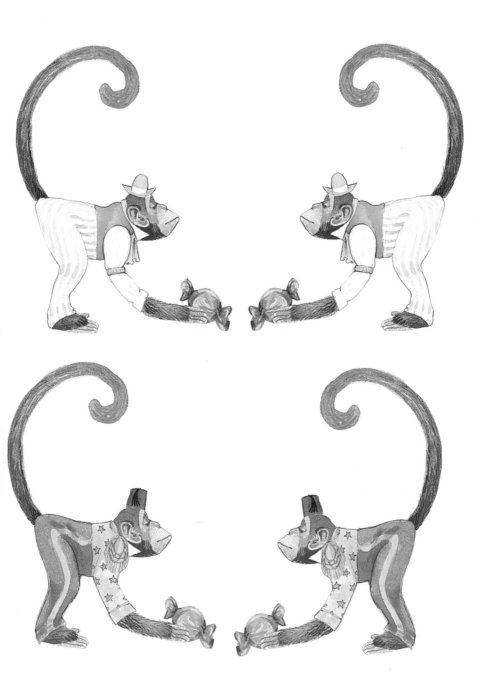

YOUR FAVOURITE COCKTAILS & TWISTS

YOUR FAVOURITE COCKTAILS & TWISTS

YOUR FINAL THOUGHTS

YOUR FINAL THOUGHTS

YOUR FINAL THOUGHTS

YOUR FINAL THOUGHTS

PARLOUR GAMES

Playing games encourages laughter and closeness and helps push day-to-day thoughts and worries to one side as the players become engulfed in the moment. Parlour games are a wonderful form of escapism and are perfect for a tea party. Below are a few of my favourites.

Guess the clothing era

Ask everyone to wear a piece of vintage clothing to your party. Each person must do a bit of research to ascertain the correct era or year of their clothing beforehand – for example, they might plump for a 1960s waistcoat. The rest of the guests then try to guess the vintage of the piece of clothing.

Guess the musical era

You'll need two teams and around five songs for each team. You'll need to know the year of release for each one. Practise the songs and some dance moves to showcase them. The other team get a point for naming the song, a point for the era and a bonus point for the actual year.

Unconventional poker

Each player is dealt one card, face down. Without peeking at it, they display the card to all the other players by licking it and sticking it to their forehead, facing outwards. This is followed by a round of betting. Players attempt to guess if they have the highest card based on the distribution of visible cards and how the other players are betting. Betting continues until players fold as they think they have a lower card than the other players. When there are only two people remaining, the winner is the person with the highest card.

Charades

Players split into two teams. A member of one team mimes the title of a film, play, book, song or musical, provided by the other team in secret, to the other members of their own team, who try to guess the title from the clues provided. There is a time limit and a number of standard gestures. Many different versions of the rules exist, so always try to agree them before you start.

Are you there, Moriarty?

Two players at a time participate in a duel. Each player is blindfolded and given something that is unlikely to hurt as a weapon, such as a rolled-up newspaper. The players start off either lying on their fronts, head to head, with a metre or so between them, or holding one another's hand in a handshake. One player asks 'Are you there, Moriarty?'. The other answers 'Yes', and the duel begins. The aim of the game is to avoid being hit by the other player. The first player to get hit is out and, when this happens, another player steps in and the game continues.

The list game

This is a memory game. The first player says 'I went to the shop and bought…' an item beginning with the letter A. The next player repeats this, then adds an item beginning with B, and so on. Test your memory skills after a few gin cocktails!

HAIR BASICS

YOU WILL NEED

Kirby grips

Curl clips

Hairpins (preferably the same colour as your hair)

Good-quality bristle hairbrush

Tail comb

Velcro rollers
It's good to have a variety of sizes to get different styles, but if you only buy one size make it 3cm (1¼in) in diameter.

Hair mousse
(preferably for curls)

Hair pomade or wax

Setting lotion
It's best to decant this into a spray bottle. The stronger ones I would recommend you use need watering down to one part lotion to two parts water.

Medium curling tongs

Hairdryer or hood dryer
Hood dryers are still widely available at major retailers or on the internet. Alternatively, you can get a fabric hood dryer which attaches to your regular hairdryer.

Hairspray
(the strongest you can find)

Sectioning clips

Shine spray

WHAT YOU NEED TO KNOW

When using rollers, or pin curling, always roll the hair horizontally as this gives your hair the most beautiful vintage curl. If you're having trouble making sure that the ends of your hair are wrapped securely around a roller or in a pin curl, use the narrow end of a tail comb to tuck the ends under the rest of the hair on the roller or into the pin curl. If you take your curlers out and you vaguely resemble a French poodle, don't panic! The secret to these styles is all in the brushing – lots of it.

PiN CURLS

If you don't have the time to use rollers, setting your hair with pin curls can have equally wonderful results. Apply a liberal amount of mousse to dry hair and follow the sectioning stages for the Classic Set (*see* pages 146–149) while your curling tongs heat up. Taking rectangular sections of hair no wider than 1cm (½in), pull the hair taut at a 45-degree angle. While holding the tongs horizontally, wind the hair around the tongs, making sure it is distributed evenly along the barrel. To avoid the dreaded 'fish-hook' effect so commonly experienced with curling tongs, gently release the tong clamp and slide the tongs along the hair until the ends are securely tucked in the clamp. Wind the hair under towards the head, rather than over. Hold the tongs in place for around 20 seconds then gently release the clamp and remove the tongs. While the hair is still hot, wind it around your forefinger, keeping the curl horizontal and use a kirby grip to secure.

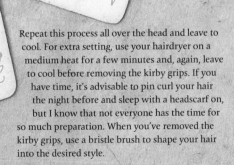

Repeat this process all over the head and leave to cool. For extra setting, use your hairdryer on a medium heat for a few minutes and, again, leave to cool before removing the kirby grips. If you have time, it's advisable to pin curl your hair the night before and sleep with a headscarf on, but I know that not everyone has the time for so much preparation. When you've removed the kirby grips, use a bristle brush to shape your hair into the desired style.

THE
CLASSIC
SET

This timeless style works on hair of all lengths and most types, and you can adjust the type of curl or wave you want by using different-sized rollers. There are various ways to achieve the Classic Set, with some people preferring to style their hair from wet and others from dry. There are those who prefer to use setting lotion and others who prefer mousse; some use Velcro rollers and a hood dryer and others like to pin curl. It really is about experimenting and finding out what works best for your hair type and length and what kind of curl you want. The traditional method was a wet set with a hood dryer, which not only gives a better hold, but the whole process is ridiculously glamorous and fun, and that's just what us vintage girls are all about.

STEP 1 After washing your hair, blow-dry with a hairdryer until it's about 80–90 per cent dry. Spray your hair liberally with setting lotion all over and comb through to ensure even coverage. If any part of the hair is dry, it will set unevenly and potentially drop very quickly.

STEP 2 Part your hair using a tail comb into a front and back section from one ear to the other across the crown of the head. Divide the front section into two, keeping a side parting. The two front sections should be about the width of the roller you'll be using.

STEP 3 Starting on either side, take a rectangular section of hair about 1cm (½in) deep and, starting at a 45-degree angle away from the wrapping direction, wrap the hair around the Velcro roller horizontally, rolling under, not over. Make sure that you hold the hair taut while rolling. Velcro rollers will generally stay in place themselves, but for extra security I use curl clips or kirby grips as well. Continue this process on both side sections, ensuring that all the rollers are horizontal and as close to your head as possible.

STEP 4 Part the hair at the back into two sections vertically and repeat the process until all your hair is set in rollers.

STEP 5 Now comes the easy part: spend 45–60 minutes (depending on the thickness of your hair) under a hood dryer. You can use this time to paint your nails, do your make-up or just relax. For a set that will last for days, set your hair in the evening, sleep in your rollers (the things we do for glamour!) and wear a headscarf all day before taking the rollers out in the evening.

STEP 6 Make sure that you let your hair cool for about 15 minutes before removing the rollers. At this stage you will be wondering where your Lana Turner-style curls are, as you will be looking more like Shirley Temple, but fear not. Using your bristle brush, give your hair a good, thorough brushing. Now you may start to look like that French poodle mentioned earlier. Using the palms of your hands, apply a little styling pomade or wax through the lengths. Then, by brushing a little more lightly, start shaping the hair, even using your fingers, until you have achieved a look that you are happy with. Finish your style with a strong hairspray.

Make-up
and Make-out

A flirty flick and a ruby lip is all it takes to make every day a glamorous one. Just have a look at the colour palette and follow these simple steps for the perfect vintage look.

Create a clean flawless complexion by covering blemishes and under-eye circles with concealer. Use green concealer to balance out red imperfections.

Use a liquid or cream foundation that matches your skin tone. Apply with a brush for even coverage. If using liquid, always squeeze onto the back of your hand first, to avoid going overboard.

Use an eyebrow pencil or angled brush and eyeshadow to fill in your brows. The vintage eyebrow is strong, sculpted and dark. The brow should start above the inner corner of the eye and extend past the outer edge.

Next, use a neutral eyeshadow to cover the entire eyelid before lining the socket crease with a darker brown. Use the palette to experiment with day and evening shades.

To create the liquid eyeliner flick, close one eye and draw as close to the lash line as possible in one swoop, extending beyond the edge of the eye to create the flick. You may find it easier to pull the side of the eye taut. 'Practice makes perfect' should be your mantra.

If you want a beauty spot use your eyeliner to do this, and experiment with positioning.

Crack a smile and dust the 'apples' of your cheeks with blush.

Use a loose or compact powder to finish off the look. This is an essential stage that will seal your make-up and complete your flawless face.

Next, use a black mascara to extend and curl your lashes – using curlers beforehand is optional. If it's an evening event, fake eyelashes are essential.

To create the perfect pout moisturize your lips with balm. Carefully draw around the lips' edges with a lip pencil. Using a matching colour, fill in your lips with a brush and blend with the pencil. To make sure you won't get any on your teeth, suck your thumb and then pucker your lips on a piece of tissue to blot off any excess.

Job done!

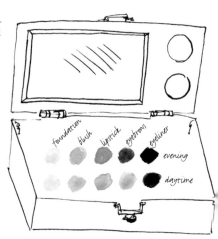

Trial Your Look

Capture what you love - find your style

WHO CAME?

Did they bring you a gift? Write it here... it's so easy to forget with all the excitement! And it's so nice to mention this in a thank you!

VINTAGE PATISSERIE THANK YOU

ARIOTEK *ariotek.co.uk* For being the best web-hosting company I've ever come across. Drew and Colin, you are both amazing!

BARNET & LAWSON *bltrimmings.com* For being the only haberdashery I'll ever need to go to. London is worth a visit just for you.

BENEFIT COSMETICS *benefitcosmetics.com* For making the 'Big Beautiful Eyes' product.

BETHAN SOANES *bethan-soanes.co.uk* For being stunning, and for being there for the VP every time we need you! Lovely seeing your career take off!

BEYOND RETRO *beyondretro.com* For being a one-stop for vintage clothes and accessories and where most of my wardrobe is from!

CAROLINE ALBERTI AT OCTOPUS I have four books' worth of thank yous to make to you! Thank you for your relentless hard work on these beauties. I honestly don't know how we managed to get this book turned around in time. You are like the Father Christmas of books – a miracle worker!

CAROLYN WHITEHORNE *toniandguy.com* For your support, encouragement and for being a friend.

CASS STAINTON For understanding me and throwing some pretty amazing parties! I miss you!

CLIFF FLUET *lewissilkin.com* For becoming my friend, for your support and encouragement, for understanding what I want to achieve. Cliff, you are amazing.

COMPANY MAGAZINE *company.co.uk* For your support.

DANDY DAN Dan, you are a true gentleman. I know you work in-house now, but I'll always hold you to that coffee we talked about!

DAVID CARTER *alacarter.com* For being a loyal, eccentric dandy. Your creativity has no limits. P.S. I think I did sell more books than you? :-)

DEBORAH MEADEN *deborahmeaden.com* For believing in me and providing me with a stepping stone to grow my business. Thank you.

DENHAM PRODUCTIONS To Jill, for being a bit mental and for loving Arthur!

DENISE BATES AT OCTOPUS For being so supportive in a tough year. You are an amazing lady!

ELEANOR MAXFIELD AT OCTOPUS For commissioning the first book! For totally getting the second book! For making miracles happen with the third! For being by my side and supporting me every step of the way. You believe, you care and you are always fair. That totally rhymes! So happy you have become my friend.

ELNETT HAIRSPRAY *loreal-paris.co.uk/styling/elnett.aspx* What would we do without you?

EMMA PERRIS *emmaperris.co.uk* For the wonderful massages you give, for your support and for being my mate!

FLEUR BRITTEN *fleurbritten.moonfruit.com* For being fabulous and supportive. It was lovley seeing you as a beautiful mum!

FLEUR DE GUERRE *diaryofavintagegirl.com* For being a gorgeously talented ghetto vintage lady. For jumping in when I have needed you and for being a good friend. Please stop being so fabulous.

FRASER DOHERTY & ANTHONY McGINLEY *superjam.co.uk* For being business inspirations. I'm always so proud to say you are my friends!

GRAZIA *graziadaily.co.uk* For your support.

HARPER'S BAZAAR *harpersbazaar.com* For your support.

HAZEL HOLTHAM *ragandbow.com* For being an amazing business woman and friend. Hazel, you are a beauty inside and out, and it's been a joy watching your business develop and even more of a joy to watch you fall in love – I'm actually going to get my hat soon!

HOTCAKE KITTY *hotcakekitty.com* For being such a hard-working beauty! I'm glad you're on my team!

JOHN MOORE *rsmtenon.com* For training me when I was 18, for helping at every step of the way, for caring and being a true friend.

KAREN BAKER AT OCTOPUS For creating a bible of press that only a person who cares and has drive could achieve! You do the work of an entire team and I could not ask for more. Thank you for being so wonderful. I'm looking forward to 'press-ing' this book, just so we get to talk more!

KATHY AT PAST PERFECT *pastperfect.com* For having a brilliant company that sells amazing music!

KATIE, POPPY & RICHARD *whatkatiedid.com* For being the first to make a real business out of vintage – you are the leader, OH KATIE! For being my friend and inspiring me. Thanks for your support. Let's take over the world ;-)

LADY LUCK *ladyluckclub.co.uk* For being the first vintage dance club in London and both being so fabulous.

LAURA ASHLEY *lauraashley.com* For being a fabulous client with a fabulous team and brand.

LAURA CHERRY For being such a beauty, inside and out. You are an inspiring lady, hard-working, and I'm proud that you are achieving your dream. Thank you for being part of the team.

LAUREN CRAIG *thinkingflowers.org.uk* For caring where your flowers come from, for being so talented and for being my friend.

LEANNE BRYAN AT OCTOPUS Thank you for caring and being so gentle and calming. I could not ask for more from an editor!

158

LIAN HIRST *tracepublicity.com* For having the best fashion PR label in town, FOR BEING DOROTHY'S GODMOTHER! Thank you for supporting and being an amazing friend. You have totally spoilt me, Dorothy and Arthur this year. We are so lucky to have you and Paul in our lives.

LIPSTICK & CURLS *lipstickandcurls.net* For your inspiring hairstyles and for being amazingly talented. Thank you for your support and for being my friend and letting your whole family be in this book!

MAC COSMETICS *maccosmetics.com* For creating the perfect look. What would a girl do without her Ruby Woo?

MARGARET AT VINTAGE HEAVEN *vintageheaven.co.uk* Margaret! You are the most amazing woman that roams the planet! Your positivity fills my heart. In fact, Dick is quite sure it's changed our lives. We truly love you! You have spoilt us this year – thanks for being such a caring friend.

MEHMET AT SIMPLY FRESH I'm so proud of you!

NAOMI AND VINTAGE SECRETS *vintagesecret.com* For your support and love of vintage!

NINA BUTKOVICH-BUDDEN *ninashairparlour.com* Oh Nina! Leader of the vintage hair pack! You are so talented, I miss you!

OCTOPUS TEAM For all being so lovely and believing in this book!

PATRICK AT VALUE MY STUFF *valuemystuff.com* For being inspiring and having such a great business.

PETER & SASHA For always bringing amazing life to every party! I wish I could have you more!

PETE KATSIAOUNIS *inkandmanners.com* For doing the illustrations for all my websites! You go beyond the call of duty.

ROKIT *rokit.co.uk* Thank you for being the first vintage shop I ever bought anything in! Imogen Excell, they are lucky to have you and so is Pandora!

ROSIE ALIA JOHNSON *rosiealia.blogspot.co.uk* For being a beautiful spirit and part of the team. For bringing the first clothes collection to life – it will happen! And for making such lovely hair flowers! You are a very talented beauty.

SALES AT OCTOPUS Becs, Kevin, Siobhan, Terry, Vanessa (listed in alphabetic order)… Sales! Thank you for getting the book out into the big wide world! You do me proud and I know you talk about the book with passion. Thank you!

SARAH KEEN *curiousmenagerie.co.uk* For being so bloody supportive and brilliant at everything you do! I've loved watching your taxidermy classes grow and I've loved working with you and having you as my crafty Girl Friday on all the books Xx

SHARON TRICKETT *minniemoons.com* For being incredibly hard-working and talented and utterly fabulous. It's been lovely watching you grow Minni Moons.

SIMONE HADFIELD *miss-turnstiles.blogspot.co.uk* Where does one start?! Thank you for throwing yourself into the Vintage Patisserie and investing your heart! It's been brilliant watching your journey as entrepreneur begin and I'm looking forward to seeing you grow. I know you will get everything you wish for.

SOPHIA HUNT AT BELLADONNA BEAUTY PARLOUR I'm so proud and happy you were part of the team! You are an incredibly talented lady and I wish you luck in whatever your future holds.

SOPHIE LAURIMORE *factualmanagement.com* For being a very supportive agent! For understanding my life. It's been great growing our businesses togther. Thank you to you and your family for being so fabulous and for being on the front cover!

STYLIST *stylist.co.uk* For your support.

SUCK & CHEW *suckandchew.co.uk* For having the best sweet shop in East London.

SUSIE AND THE LUNA & CURIOUS TEAM *lunaandcurious. blogspot.com* Susie. Your creativity inspires me. You must see this in everything I do now. Thank you for bringing the Luna & Curious people together and for your 24/7 support!

TIME OUT LONDON *timeout.com/london* For your support.

TOP SHELF JAZZ *topshelfjazz.com* Always there to perform a treat! Thank you for always being amazing at everything I have booked you for.

UNCLE ROY'S *uncleroys.co.uk* For selling edible flowers (roses) and having the most fabulous company!

VINTAGE VICTORY *vintagevictory.com* G & K – how do you get to be so wonderful in your field and be parents?! I take my vintage hat off to you.

YASIA WILIAMS AT OCTOPUS For so much I don't know where to begin. Firstly, for your dedication and hard work. For your love of every project. For understanding what I want in your sleep! I don't think I could work with anyone else – well, want to, for sure! Your insight and advice as a working mum has been incredible. I love you YW!

YUKI SUGIURA *yukisugiura.com* For caring and being so talented and creative. Work is no meant to be this fun. You understand exactly what makes my mind work and, together, we are a great team. Your food photography makes me smile like a Cheshire cat.

Angel Adoree Thank You

ANDREYA TRIANA Thank you for filling my life with music and love and endless praise! If I could sing, I'd ask for a voice like yours.

BOBBY NICHOLLS & LORD IAN My best party boys! I just need to party more! Which now needs planning! Please can we make this happen?

CHRISTINA LAU I always feel very emotional when I need to express my thank yous to you. Your love and continued belief in me, teaching me how to bake, helping with websites, business problems and, now, endless mum advice… you are my friend and my mentor and one of the few people I can turn to for help. I now have a new level of apprecation for everything you have done, as you did lots as a new mum! I love you darlin'.

DARREN WHELEN My oldest friend. Thank you for your love and support and for reminding me to stop every now and again! Congratulations on your new life! I'm so happy for you. I need to meet Princess Nahla.

ELIZABETH OSBOURNE Thank you for caring and teaching me to read! Your memory has never been forgotten.

GAIA FACCHINI (MOUTHFUL O' JAM) You slipped into our lives and it's like you were always here. Thank you.

GRANDMA & GRANDAD (RIP) You were dream grandparents and I'm so lucky to have had you both. Your love for your extending family knows no bounds and I can't wait until Arthur Donald and Dorothy Francis grow up to know how wonderful their great-grandparents were.

JIM & DAVID WALKER Arthur's gorgeous 'non-religious' Godfather! Thank you for being so friggin' wonderful and managing to be in London for everything special this year! We are very lucky to have you in our lives and have been so spoilt by you and David. I can't wait for Arthur to get to know you and see your beauty inside and out. I love you.

JOHN, JULIE & KATIE WALKER My second family! Thank you for the love I receive all the way from over the pond! Not to mention taking me around all the vintage shops every time I come to visit!

JOSEPH YIANNA For your friendship and support and for being so fabulous!

JUDITH BIFFIGER For sharing your world, inspiring me with music and love and being the gentlest, sweetest person ever!

KATE & JOE SKULLY For making me laugh until my sides split, for being bloody fabulous and for the love and support you have always shown.

LEALEA JONES For singing like an angel, for your open heart and for knowing that hard work pays off. Ms Jones, you are an inspiration to me and your peers around you. Hackney is a lucky place.

LEAH PRENTICE For being the second Vintage Patisserie team member! And for being my mate and causing me to laugh too many times. Mwah!

LEE BEHAN Life's a pitch and I'll never forget it! Thank you for being inspiring and supportive!

LEO CHADBURN I'll always remember how we met. I was sitting in a bar with my feet on the table and you approached me and said, 'your shoes are fabulous, would you like to party?' I'm not quite sure if that's how it happened, but that's what I'll go with. Fourteen years of friendship and I love you so much. Your mum was proud of what an amazing son she has.

MEL PATEL For being my mate and the only DJ I'd ever employ.

MUM & DAD I've always thanked you for the years I remember, but I have a new appreciation now for all the years I don't remember! You are wonderful parents and amazing grandparents. I can see the way you look at Arthur and Dorothy and know that's how you looked at me – unconditional love. I'm the person I am because of you both. I know you tell me how proud you are of me, but I am of you both, too.

NAN For being you, nan – I love you.

NATASHA For your love and support.

PAUL For being a great brother and a great dad! I'm looking forward to Arthur and Dorothy getting to know their Uncle Paul. You are a kid at heart and that's why kids fall in love with you!

SARAH, LEROY, HENRY & OSCAR Thank you for going beyond the call of friendship and believing in me. In your words, I can't wait for our families to grow up together. Thank you for being there and holding my hand!!!

SEYMOUR NURSE When I see your name, I smile. Your kind words live in my heart and I'll love you forever, Peter Pan!

TAJ CAMBRIDGE Every year feels as if we have achieved a lifetime of dreams? I see us both take steps on our journey every day, but we will never get to the end because we want to pack our lives to the brim with tales and experiences. I'm loving our journey. I love you.

TATE & ANTHONY You two lovebirds are so inspiring with your business ventures! I love being around you and lerning new stuff! *www.anytodo. com* is genius and that's purely because of you both.

THE STRAWBRIDGES It's worrying that I feel so at home with you because you are all wonderfully crazy! I could not feel more loved and it's magical to see us grow as a family. Arthur and Dorothy are so loved, they may just pop. I love you all.

VAL & CO. AT THE PALM TREE For giving me the best nights of my life and for being such a lovely family!

VICKI, ROSY & THEO For your love and support, and for the party years! I've loved seeing your family grow and I can't wait for our families to grow up togther. Thank you for being so generous on every level. I love you.